A New World Order
Can It Bring Security to the World's People?

———

Essays on Restructuring the United Nations

Front page cover is a photo of a Guinea Bissau mother and child listening to an address being made by Chairman of a UN Mission to her area. Photo credit: United Nations/Y. Nagata. 1972.

Editor: Walter Hoffmann

Assistant Editor: Scott Hoffman

Published by:

WORLD FEDERALIST ASSOCIATION
418 7th Street Southeast
Washington, DC 20003
(202) 546-3950

September, 1991

This book is dedicated to the children of all nations, that they may live in a world where peace, security, and a clean environment are guaranteed.

ACKNOWLEDGEMENTS

The World Federalist Association (WFA) acknowledges the debt and gratitude it owes to all of the authors who contributed to this book. The expertise of the outside contributors was invaluable. WFA also had the good fortune of benefiting from four excellent summer interns (three in the Washington office and one in our Pittsburgh office) who threw themselves into the project and together contributed eight of the articles. We apologize publicly to all of the authors for the editing and condensing that we did.

We also wish to thank Marilyn Hill and Suzanne Picard who "word processed" and proofread the manuscripts, deciphered numerous editing changes, and helped with the layout. Both voluntarily worked extra days beyond their regular work weeks in order to get the book completed in time for WFA's community consensus outreach program. Without Marilyn's and Suzanne's extra efforts, the book would not have been ready.

I also wish to thank Scott Hoffman (no relation), who helped me considerably with the editing, and Tony Allen, who helped find many of the pictures and graphics. In this connection, we especially thank the United Nations Office of Public Information for lending us many of the photographs that appear on the pages that follow.

Lastly, we want to register our deepest gratitude to the anonymous World Federalist couple whose major contribution to WFA in July made the publication of this book possible.

Walter Hoffmann
Executive Director

September, 1991

ISBN No. 1-880533-02-2

INTRODUCTION

President Bush brought the term back into current usage at the outset of the War in the Gulf; but the concept of a "new world order" is an old one. It is enshrined in the preamble to the Charter of the United Nations, with its determination "to save succeeding generations from the scourge of war..., to reaffirm faith in fundamental human rights..., to promote social progress and better standards of life in larger freedom..." There is something in the idea of a world recreated free from war, pollution, injustice and poverty that is tremendously inspiring; it appeals to a drive, rooted in our culture at least as far back as the Renaissance, to seek perfection in this world. Mr. Bush's phrase had power because it touched this taproot of inspiration.

From their beginning in 1947, World Federalists have distinguished themselves from the rest of the peace and justice movement by insisting that the millennial vision in phrases like "new world order" can only be realized through governmental structures. Our faith is not in human moral perfectibility, at least not in the short run, but in systems of governance that can regulate conflict between human beings and keep it at a manageable level. It's all too possible that President Bush did not imagine, in his use of "new world order," either the millennial goals suggested above or the structural means that World Federalists advocate. But to debate the President's policy is not our main objective here. Rather, we want to use the President's phrase with all its idealistic implications and show how the structural approach can bring step by step realization of the ideal.

This book examines most major factors that might be changed under a new world order, including armaments, dispute resolution, environment, development and human rights. It looks at potential ways of strengthening the United Nations, including the transformation of the UN Charter into a constitution for a global federation. Many of the views expressed are not official policies of the World Federalist Association, but all reflect our structural approach. Some of the articles have been edited so that, without violating the opinions of the writers, they hold more closely to the purposes and format of this book.

As we prepared to go to press, news came of a coup in the Soviet Union. If the coup brings about a lasting reversal of the liberalization there, some of our authors' celebration of an "opportunity in the East" may lose its appropriateness. On the other hand, the coup underlines the danger all humanity faces in an ungoverned world.

This book was intended most immediately as a study guide for World Federalist chapters and other local organizations interested in world order. But we hope that it will also make a significant contribution to the larger debate about what changes in world order are both just and feasible.

Scott Hoffman
National Field Director

TABLE OF CONTENTS

Part One: Security and Dispute Settlement in a Nuclear World

Part Two: Building the Institutions for Global Governance

Part Three: Environment, Economics, and Human Rights

Part Four: Alternative Paths to a New World Order

CONTRIBUTORS

ANTHONY ALLEN was the Student Programs Director of the World Federalist Association (WFA) from 1988 to 1991. He is a member of the national board of WFA.

JOSEPH BARATTA is a scholar of the history of the world federalist movement and the author of several monographs on aspects of world order for the Center for UN Reform Education.

GERALD BIESECKER-MAST is a doctoral candidate in Communications at the University of Pittsburgh. He spent the summer of 1991 interning at WFA's Pittsburgh office.

KATHRYN DAMM, a junior at St. Mary's College, South Bend, Indiana, was an intern at WFA's national office during the summer of 1991.

ARAM FUCHS, a senior at Union College, Schenectady, New York, interned during the summer of 1991 at WFA's national office.

RON GLOSSOP, Chair of the Peace Studies Program and professor of Philosophical Studies at Southern Illinois University, is the author of the book Confronting War. He is the First Vice-President and Chair of the Publications Committee of WFA, as well as Chair of WFA's St. Louis chapter.

JOHN HOLDEN is the former President of the Adult Education Association for the USA. He is chair of WFA's Advisory Board and a member of the Executive and Administrative Committees.

RICHARD HUDSON is Director of the Center for War/Peace Studies in New York City.

MIRIAM LEVERING is former Executive Secretary of the Ocean Education Project and a member of WFA's Advisory Board.

JOHN LOGUE is Director of the Common Heritage Institute of Villanova University in Pennsylvania. He is Vice-President of WFA and the author of numerous monographs and articles on world federalist subjects.

BRYAN MACPHERSON, an attorney at the U.S. Department of Energy, is Recording Secretary and Newsletter Editor of WFA's Washington, D.C. chapter.

CHARLES PRICE is former President of the American Chemical Society and current President of WFA.

BARBARA WALKER is Vice-Chair of the Executive Committee and Chair of the School Liaison Committee of WFA. She is also editor of The World Federalist Reader.

MARK YAKICH is a senior at Illinois Wesleyan. He interned at WFA's national office in the summer of 1991 and is currently studying in Vienna.

JACK YOST is UN Office Director of the World Federalist Movement.

Part One
SECURITY & DISPUTE SETTLEMENT IN A NUCLEAR WORLD

1. The Need for an International Disarmament Organization

by Charles C. Price

If we do indeed seek world peace with justice under law, then national disarmament is one essential requirement. The assertion of every nation that it has the right to acquire and use weapons of mass destruction to further its own interest is morally and economically unacceptable. Efforts to control and reduce national armaments is a step in the right direction.

President John F. Kennedy asked John J. McCloy to undertake negotiations with the Soviet Union on how to reduce and eliminate the threat of nuclear war. He and Valerian Zorin, USSR Deputy Foreign Minister in 1961, proposed a "Joint Statement of Agreed Principles for Disarmament Negotiations" which was endorsed by a vote of 125-0 by the U.N. General Assembly. This revolutionary document proposed (a) the stepwise elimination of all national military establishments and (b) "establishment of reliable procedures for the peaceful settlement of disputes" under the U.N.

Paragraph 6 of the McCloy-Zorin statement calls for "an international disarmament organization including all parties to the agreement" to be "created within the framework of the United Nations."

"This international disarmament organization and its inspectors should be assured unrestricted access without veto to all places, as necessary for the purpose of effective verification."

The important governing structure and financing for this inspection agency was not specified but must provide it with adequate autonomy and authority. Questions of this nature are currently at issue in the U.N. inspection of Iraqi military facilities as mandated by the cease fire agreement.

The creation of an International Disarmament Organization was formally proposed by the 1978 U.N. General Assembly Special Session on Disarmament. Such an agency would have a useful role for "third party" monitoring of existing arms control agreements. It could assist in the process of reaching further agreements. Its experience could be helpful in developing inspection procedures for "complete disarmament in a peaceful world," as proposed by McCloy and Zorin.

For the long years of the "cold war," it was very difficult to see how the goal of disarmament could be achieved. With the revolutionary changes in the Soviet Union, the demise of the Berlin Wall, and the burgeoning unification of Europe, realistic progress may now be possible. Progress will, of course, require progress in giving the U.N. enough authority to provide for national security from armed attack. A fundamental principle of global law must therefore be absolute respect for national boundaries. Any present or future disputes over them must be resolved by mutual agreement, by binding arbitration or by binding decision of the International Court of Justice. Many current boundary disputes are related to issues of national military security and will, of course, become much less significant in a disarmed and peaceful world.

Why has the U.N. so far failed to achieve its goals? They are indeed nobly stated in the preamble, yet we remain in a world threatened by the most destructive weapons of mass destruction ever created. McCloy and Zorin called for agreement to "strengthen institutions for maintaining peace and the settlement of disputes by peaceful means." This is a critical requirement for "general and complete disarmament in a peaceful world."

If the U.N. is to be effective and acceptable in this role it must be restructured and strengthened with defined and agreed authority to

(a)   raise its own revenues directly, for example, by taxes on international travel, communication and commerce;

(b)   make binding decisions by a responsible majority voting system based at least in part on population and economic factors of member states;

(c)   enforce such binding decisions based mainly on nonviolent coercion applied directly to individuals as well as member states who break such United Nations law but with limited police power sufficient to maintain international order and to apprehend international lawbreakers in a disarmed world;

(d)   endow the International Court of Justice, and any subsidiary or regional U.N. courts, with compulsory jurisdiction to make binding decisions in disputes over international treaties and over charges of breaking United Nations law.

Any agreement to establish such significant authority in the U.N. almost certainly will require

(a)   a clear statement of legal principles limiting improper exercise of U.N. authority by providing for guarantees of basic human rights and freedoms, and

(b)   arrangements for use of a significant fraction of the resources now devoted to war and military establishments to world economic development.

The U.N. is in fact currently involved in exercising the right to intervene in Iraq to protect the human rights of the Kurds.

In summary, for significant progress toward disarmament, the U.N. must be given authority to provide global security, promote human rights, and protect the global environment.

1A. The Potential for a UN Verification Agency

by Aram Fuchs

During the first two decades of the United Nations, disarmament negotiations were deadlocked because of the tensions of the Cold War. The West charged that the East wanted "disarmament without control" and the East charged that the West wanted "control without disarmament." In the early sixties, both sides began to display a bit more flexibility, and minimal arms control measures, accompanied by weak verification provisions and strong reliance on limited surveillance by the superpowers, became possible.

More recently, under the leadership of President Gorbachev, there was a major shift in Soviet policy. The Soviet Union may now be willing to accept far ranging international inspections -- in certain cases even before negotiations are completed. Because of the need for the Soviet Union to transfer economic resources from the military to its consumer segment of society, there is a window of opportunity for peace.

In 1989, the Soviet Union and the United States, for the first time, jointly co-sponsored a resolution in the General Assembly aimed at strengthening "the role and effectiveness of the United Nations in maintaining international peace and security." Because of these and other fundamental changes, it may now be possible for the international community to embark on a path of progressive disarmament "under effective international control."

In today's context, control means treaty verification, compliance promotion and to a certain extent treaty enforcement. The Non-Aligned Movement recently adopted the proposal for "the establishment of an integrated multilateral verification system."

Because of East/West tensions, almost all of the earlier disarmament proposals were never developed in sufficient detail. There was one important exception: the International Atomic Energy Agency (IAEA) -- which was proposed by President Eisenhower in 1953 and which came into being in 1957.

The International Atomic Energy Agency promotes the peaceful uses of atomic energy and implements safeguards to verify that materials used by participating states are not diverted for military purposes. Eisenhower's primary concern at the time was to begin creating mechanisms of international inspections for arms control and disarmament. But it was not until ten years after it was created that the IAEA actually acquired a role in the implementation of an arms control treaty: the Treaty of Tlatelolco. Subsequently, the agency was employed to help verify two other arms control treaties -- the Non-Proliferation Treaty and the South Pacific Nuclear Free Zone Treaty.

Another significant arms verification institution, an International Satellite Monitoring Agency (ISMA), was proposed by the President of France in 1978. The

H-Bomb detonation, Marshall Islands, 1952. Photo credit: United Nations U.S.I.A.

idea was examined in a UN study in 1981 which concluded, among other things, that ISMA could make a valuable contribution to arms control verification, and that nothing in international law would prohibit if from carrying out its proposed monitoring functions.

At the time, both superpowers expressed opposition to the idea of an ISMA because it represented an encroachment on their monopoly of satellite reconnaissance information. However, the Soviet Union has since come out in favor of the concept and has even suggested that ISMA become a part of a larger UN monitoring and verification agency.

The two superpowers have now dramatically reversed their former positions regarding the establishment of a UN verification agency which was proposed in 1988 by the Six Nation Initiative (Argentina, Greece, India, Mexico, Sweden, and Tanzania). The Soviet Union, which previously opposed almost all inspections, is apparently willing to accept wide-ranging

and intrusive inspections and is in favor of a strong verification role for the United Nations. At the third UN Special Session on Disarmament in 1988, Soviet Foreign Minister Shevardnadze proposed the creation of an "international monitoring and verification agency" under the auspices of the United Nations. In the 1988 regular session, he cited "the acute need for new mechanisms of verification and control" and proposed that a worldwide seismic monitoring system and an International Satellite Monitoring Agency (ISMA) could become part of the agency.

The United States, which proposed the extensive Baruch plan in the 1940's to control atomic weapons, now opposes proposals to create a UN verification agency. It cast the single negative vote against the 1988 verification resolution which initiated a Secretary-General's study. In explaining its vote, the United States expressed the view that any verification arrangement must be developed and agreed upon by the negotiating parties. The United States did not see how the Secretary-General could undertake an in-depth study of the role of the United Nations in the field of verification in the abstract, in the absence of the parameters that specific agreements might provide for such a role in individual cases.

The primary function of a UN verification agency (UNVA) would be to promote and enhance verification and compliance with any number of arms control initiatives -- including multilateral disarmament and arms limitation treaties, as well as confidence-building and unilateral measures undertaken by countries.

Also, by maintaining a nucleus of international expertise before treaties are signed, verification will be available when it is most needed: at the beginning of the treaty implementation. Just as the safeguards system of the International Atomic Energy Agency (IAEA) was in existence before the 1968 Non-Proliferation Treaty was signed and could quickly be extended to cover the treaty, so too a UNVA could be in place and have acquired expertise before new disarmament treaties are signed.

Before and during disarmament negotiations, the UNVA could perform preliminary inspections within states which request them. For instance, the UNVA could verify the size of certain declared arm stocks. This might serve as a welcome boost to negotiations, especially in situations where current military capabilities are a point of contention.

Many nations would prefer inspection by UN personnel rather than by agents of other states or from many different verification organizations. Even the superpowers, which have accused each other of many treaty violations, may see benefits in giving the UNVA certain responsibilities once the objectivity, efficiency, and impartiality of the agency is demonstrated.

The UNVA would allow nations which have little or no technical expertise of their own to participate in the verification process. Each nation party has a right and a need to be fully knowledgeable about all other nations' compliance with agreements they all have signed. The most universal and non-discriminatory verification mechanisms are the most desirable because they would inspire the greatest confidence and trust. Since most nations cannot afford independent monitoring, the verification of most current multilateral treaties, including both data collection and interpretation, is left largely to the superpowers.

A United Nations Verification Agency is necessary, in today's world, to meet the demands for effective multilateral arms control verification and to help build global security as we enter the twenty-first century.

Verification is often the last and technically the most difficult element of a treaty to be negotiated. Unless tried and proven methods of verification are available, verification issues could once again become stumbling blocks as they were in the past.

With the changes in the East, the opportunity to achieve a United Nations Verification Agency, however embryonic, should be seized. Bilateral arms reduction agreements between the superpowers will, for the time being, be based on adversarial inspection and surveillance, but regional and global treaties require a strong multilateral framework. Without this framework there will be unacceptably slow progress in multilateral, global disarmament.

Discussion Questions

1. Is the McCloy-Zorin Agreement's call for an International Disarmament Organization to supervise general and complete disarmament an essential element in a New World Order under Law?

2. What recourse would a stronger United Nations have if a nation were caught breaking an internationally verified arms control treaty?

3. To what extent should a UN Verification Agency be allowed to use espionage to verify treaty compliance?

4. What would happen if a nation disagreed with the conclusions of an UNVA inspection?

5. Would you have more trust in the United Nations verifying disarmament treaties or the status quo method of bilateral verification?

REFERENCES AND SUGGESTED READINGS

Barrata, Joseph Preston. **Verification and Disarmament: An International Arms Control Verification Agency or International Disarmament Organization.** Center for UN Reform Education: Washington, DC, 1988.

Dorn, Walter. "Peace-keeping Satellites: The Case for International Surveillance and Verification." **Peace Research Review,** Vol. X, No. 5 & 6. Peace Research Institute: Dundas, Canada, 1987.

Hudson, Richard. "It's Time for a UN Verification Agency." **Global Report**, No. 28, June-July 1989. Center for War/Peace Studies: New York.

Noel-Baker, Philip. **The Arms Race: A Programme for World Disarmament.** Stevens and Sons: London, 1960.

Wainhouse, David W. et al. **Arms Control Agreements: Designs for Verification and Organization.** Johns Hopkins Press: Baltimore, 1968.

2. Global Security: Should There Be a Standing United Nations Police Force?
Or a United Nations Peacekeeping Reserve?

by Kathryn Damm

Peacekeeping is the principle of non-violence projected onto a military plane. It is a force that must reconcile opposing sides without appearing to dominate the rights of those it is helping. Most of all, it requires discipline, objectivity, and leadership, all of which are important to the ceaseless supervision and political direction that the use of force entails. This definition by Sir Brian Urquhart, former UN Under-Secretary General, was the basis for UN Secretary General Dag Hammarskjold's initial peacekeeping proposal.

Peacekeeping is not specifically mentioned in the UN Charter, but rather falls between Chapter VI (pacific settlement of disputes) and VII (enforcement actions to maintain peace). Chapter VII of the UN Charter gives the Security Council the specific power to determine if there is a threat to the peace and what enforcement action to take. The Security Council can ask any and all members "for armed forces, assistance and facilities, including rights of passage, necessary for the purpose of maintaining international peace and security." The Military Staff Committee, consisting of the chiefs of staff of the five permanent members of the United Nations, is supposed to act as an advisory board to the Security Council, regulating the number and type of troops that are trained for the

UN Iran-Iraq Military Observer Group, 1988. UN photo, 17251.

UN Army.

Korea and Iraq Police Actions

There are two examples of times when the UN Charter has been "loosely interpreted" to allow police action to prevent or restrain an act of aggression. The first took place during the Korean War. North Korea invaded South Korea in June 1950. The Security Council, with the U.S.S.R. absent, moved quickly to condemn the invasion, authorized members to aid South Korea and asked the U.S. to appoint a UN Commander to be in charge of all "UN forces."

The Korean police action is similar to what happened when Iraq invaded Kuwait in August 1990. The UN Security Council condemned the invasion. Urged by the U.S. and its allies, it gave UN members the right to employ all necessary means to enforce the UN resolutions. During the Gulf War, Resolution 678 authorized the use of force in Iraq by an army made up of troops from different member nations. The result was mostly American troops with some French, Saudi, Egyptian, Indian, Moroccan, British and others thrown in.

Many have accused the U.S. of "unfairly dominating the UN." The U.S. does play a role in determining what action the U.N. will take because of its status as a permanent member of the Security Council. President Bush and Secretary of State James Baker actively lobbied other member nations for support of this resolution and were instrumental in getting the Israelis not to react aggressively to Saddam Hussein.

Unlike the Korean and Iraqi police actions, peacekeeping developed through interpretation, without express amendment, in order to respond to the changing realities of the world political scene. It has been defined as a self-defense force for those who wish to contain, prevent or terminate hostilities between or within states. It has always been a very ad hoc operation, one that developed out of crisis situations. Thus, one of its main problems lies in its ambiguous guidelines that are adapted to particular situations. It does not solve anything, but may buy time if creatively employed. The hard work comes when it is time to negotiate. Over time, different types of peacekeeping and observer missions have evolved.

Nobel Peace Prize for Peacekeeping Missions

The UN was awarded the Nobel Peace Prize in 1988 for setting up two new peacekeeping missions in Iran and Iraq and in Afghanistan. The UN currently has eight peacekeeping operations under its belt. They include: the first Emergency Force in Sinai (UNEF I) November 1956-67, the UN Operation in the Congo (ONUC) July 1960-June 1964, the UN Security Force in West New Guinea (UNSF) October 1962-April 1963, the UN Peacekeeping Force in Cyprus (UNFICYP) March 1964-present, the Second UN Emergency Force in Sinai (UNEF II) October 1973-July 1979, the UN Interim Force in Lebanon (UNIFIL) March 1978 to present, the UN Transition Assistance Group (UNTAG) April 1989-March 1990 in Namibia, and there is a most current operation in Iraq protecting the Kurds and patrolling the border between Iraq and Kuwait.

Over half a million soldiers and several thousand civilians from fifty-eight nations have served as peacekeepers since 1947; nine hundred and thirty-three have died in the field. Military observers carry only binoculars and notebooks, while the peacekeeping forces carry machine guns, which they are trained to use only if they are attacked.

Peacekeeping operations themselves normally do not guarantee a lasting peace; only the parties directly involved are thought to be able to do that. "Peacekeeping is meant to provide a suitable climate for negotiations." Thus, if a UN peacekeeping force withdraws prematurely from an explosive area, fighting can and most likely will resume. For instance, UN observers and troops are not only necessary but critical in the Golan Heights area because of the tension between Israel which has annexed the territory and Syria which has claimed it. If it weren't for the peace force there, this area would be up in arms.

Peacekeeping in Namibia

Security Council Resolution 435, which authorized a peacekeeping mission in 1978 to oversee the transfer of power in Namibia, has been a lifesaving document for many Namibians. In April of 1989, two thousand SWAPO (South West African People's Organization) troops moved across the Angola border in Namibia, an action in serious violation of the Angola-Cuba-South Africa Accords. UNTAG was hurriedly created and dispatched to the region. Unfortunately, it was deployed too late and the UN had to agree to the return of South African-led Namibian Security forces to deal with the SWAPO troops. This move created tension around the world as the South African Security troops were unnecessarily brutal in their dealings with the SWAPO troops. This is a prime example of why a UN standby force, whether military or peacekeeping, is critical. This power struggle could have been avoided had the UN immediately deployed a ready group of soldiers to Namibia.

The classic struggle has been a lack of political consensus within the Security Council in implementing resolutions/courses of action. If troops had been stationed in Namibia as a preventive measure when tensions started rising, there would not have been the possibility of a SWAPO takeover. Guidelines on the training of peacekeeping forces, the actual makeup of the force, and the question of termination of the forces are all issues that still need to be resolved by the five permanent members of the Security Council.

Six Recent Proposals for Improvement

There have been at least six recent proposals on how peacekeeping should be improved by the United Nations. The U.S. proposal, initiated by President Carter and his Secretary of State Cyrus Vance in 1978, calls for a peacekeeping reserve of earmarked national forces that would be under the authority of the Secretary General and available to the Security Council on short command. The proposal offers U.S. assistance with equipment, training the reserve, and a fund of ten million dollars for emergencies by 2005. However, it rejects the idea of a permanent standby military force. This proposal was seriously pursued for two years but dropped when Reagan came into office.

In 1988 then-Secretary Mikhail Gorbachev proposed that "a wider use be made of UN military observers and UN peacekeeping forces in disengaging the troops of warring sides and observing ceasefire and armistice agreement." The proposal outlined how to set up a multilateral center for lessening the danger of war and to provide direct communication between the UN and the capitals of the permanent members of the Security Council, including observer posts in explosive areas and a reserve of armed forces, which would be made up of some Soviet forces. The U.S. and the USSR proposals differ on only two points: the U.S. emphasizes the training of peacekeeping forces while the Soviets actually volunteer their armed troops.

The Palme Commission in 1982 introduced a common-security measure that states one can only find security in cooperation, not at each other's expense. This commission sought to limit the veto so that if a party was alerted to potential disaster, the Secretary General could appoint a fact-finding mission and with the consent of the country, could send a military observer team. If tension did arise, then the Secretary General could send a UN military force to the hostile zone to act as a visible deterrent. This proposal's profile is important to note: everything hinges on the Secretary General and his response to a crisis situation.

The United Nations Association proposal of 1985 offered the following guidelines: a) a set time period for negotiations and their acceptance of a peacekeeping mission; b) a sharing of peacekeeping expenses by all parties involved; c) a national military unit and equipment for peacekeeping reserves. This proposal does not recommend standby forces that have troops from two publicly-acknowledged enemies. Because of the end of the Cold War, this issue is not as significant as it was six years ago when this was proposed.

The Campaign for UN Reform suggests recruiting individuals to be part of a permanent force loyal to the UN and able to be deployed without the host country's invitation. The reasoning behind this proposal is that those who keep peace must have the force necessary to prevent or stop war.

Lastly, in 1989 the World Association for World Federation (now the World Federalist Movement) sought a dual national/UN general war prevention and peacekeeping role. This role would include dispatching the UN Security force in time of emergency to any country that fears aggression on the part of another country.

Peacekeeping vs. Military Force

The problem with proposals such as the ones above is a fundamental difference between a peacekeeping force and a military presence. A peacekeeping force, as a rule, is interposed between two sides with their consent and by its mere presence is in the way of any attempt at aggression by either side. A military presence involves the willingness to use physical force and weaponry to halt aggression.

The UN has struggled to discern whether a military presence is the best path to take, because it is one that is hard to back off from once begun. Using military force would also directly contradict the definition Dag Hammarskjold used in the opening paragraph to describe peacekeeping. Another quasi-definition he has given on occasion is this: "To remain calm in the face of provocation, to maintain composure when under attack, the UN troops, officers, and soldiers alike must show a special kind of courage, one that is more difficult to come by than the ordinary kind. Our UN troops have been put to the test and have emerged triumphant."

But if the world is to survive, it has been argued that we must protect peace at any cost. That cost may mean taking military action against a power-hungry dictator, such as Saddam Hussein and his invasion of Kuwait. UN Resolution 678, passed on November 29, 1990, gave the member states of the UN the power of "all necessary means" to uphold and implement Security Council Resolution 660 (which condemned Iraq's invasion of Kuwait) and all subsequent relevant resolutions. Since it did not have a standby force of its own, the UN chose to authorize UN members to send their troops to reverse the invasion of Kuwait by Saddam Hussein.

Article Two, Paragraph Seven of the Charter says: "Nothing contained in the present Charter shall authorize the UN to intervene in matters which are essentially within the domestic jurisdiction of any state or shall require the Members to submit such matters to settlement under the present Charter; but this principle shall not prejudice the application of enforcement measures under Chapter VII." This was not a problem in Kuwait because it was international. However, Article Two appears to suggest that the UN can intervene uninvited in an intrastate conflict if it meets the criteria for enforcement action under Chapter VII. Those criteria include "a threat to the peace." Is a Saddam Hussein building up his arsenal of weapons a threat to the peace? It is up to the UN to decide this and take action. Chapter VII also contemplates giving the Security Council and the Military Staff Committee operational control over all member forces committed to the action. George Bush did not like this idea in Iraq because it inhibited the active and ongoing pursuit of U.S. national interests in that conflict.

In the future, the World Federalist Movement believes that the UN should have a reliable standby force that would include military, that can be deployed at the first sign of trouble to prevent a conflict from escalating and to facilitate negotiations between the two armies involved. An unarmed or lightly armed peacekeeping force may not effectively keep the tension at an acceptable level for all involved.

New Roles for Peacekeeping

In The Future of Peacekeeping, author Indar Jit Rikhye proposes several new roles for peacekeeping forces. They include border security, confidence building measures, verification of weaponry, intervention in civil wars, humanitarian aid and security, drug interdiction and naval peacekeeping. Since border security is crucial to conflict management, peacekeeping forces could play an important role in maintaining good relations while defending a country from takeover. This might be effective in Central America, where smoldering conflicts often lead nations to seek external assistance to secure their borders. Confidence building measures, designed to alleviate fear, vulnerability, and suspicion of an opposing party, can be used to clarify sticky situations and provide a channel of communication for both sides. This could include meetings between parties, visits to the opposite sides' arsenals, and observations of military maneuvers. The concept of verification, meaning to confirm or substantiate, is a significant confidence building measure that would check on the accuracy of both sides of the story. However, verification requires agreement by both sides and a good political climate in which straightforward reports could keep everyone abreast of recent developments in economic and military matters.

Although the UN Charter is based on sovereignty of states and non-interference in member states' internal affairs, many internal conflicts threaten international peace and security, making it necessary for the UN to respond. It is at this point where a military presence might be much more effective because an escalating conflict would require some show of power or force to dissipate it. In the wake of the problem of the Kurds in Iraq, it has become painfully obvious that the need for humanitarian aid is overwhelming and must be addressed if the UN is to save lives. The UN must work at

being an impartial third party, one whose only focus is feeding the people, not making political maneuvers. Impartiality is necessary in the matter of drug interdiction, where search-and-destroy missions of drug-producing factories and fields are often politically motivated. A multilateral surveillance system, backed by an intervention force, could be most effective in dealing with international drug trafficking. Lastly, naval peacekeeping could enforce naval treaties, protect merchant ships from pirating, and keep the peace in war-torn areas such as the Persian Gulf. These roles would establish a more rigorous framework for the prevention of international disputes, with respect to the national sovereignty and dignity of each state.

UN vs. U.S. as the World's Policeman

In International Peacekeeping: History and Strengthening, Joseph Preston Baratta calls for the UN to replace the U.S. as the world's policeman. He claims that no enduring harm is done if resolution of the conflict is delayed by years, so long as war is avoided. Any increase in the military capacity of peacekeeping must go together with improvements in international authority. The success of UNTSO (UN Truce Supervision Operation) in the Middle East for forty years is one example of the effectiveness of peacekeeping.

On the other side, a UN force trained, equipped, and ready for battle against national armies might have resolved several conflicts much more quickly and in the long run been better for the region as a whole. In Cyprus, UNFICYP could have stopped and turned back the Turkish army in 1974. In the Falklands, a rapidly deployable UN force could have stopped the sudden Argentine occupation of the islands.

A mere show of force might not always suffice to keep the peace, forcing the UN to engage in war. At that moment, the UN must not fail because it would lose all credibility and prestige. Baratta calls for peacekeeping to become a true international police force that would enforce international law on individuals rather than a world armed force with the power to make war on states. He echoes Hammarskjold's theory that they must use force only in self-defense, so as to prevail by their moral presence and symbolism. However, if this presence is not taken seriously, the situation could rapidly become chaotic and preventable deaths could occur. It may be more sound to plan for the prevention of a conflict than to sit around waiting for it to happen and then dealing with the logistics.

Discussion Questions

1) Should all members of the UN be asked to allocate a portion of their armed forces for UN peacekeeping free of charge?

2) Is the use of military force by the UN ever justified?

3) Until world federation is achieved, should the UN have a standby military force?

4) How can the UN enforce laws against individuals in a world of sovereign states?

5) Do you agree with Baratta or with the WAWF proposal concerning the need for an emergency military force which could be deployed and used to stop aggression?

6) Is a nonmilitary symbolic presence, such as UN peacekeepers, enough to prevent a conflict?

REFERENCES AND SUGGESTED READING

Baratta, Joseph. **International Peacekeeping: History and Strengthening.** The Center for UN Reform. November 1989.

Rikhye, Indar Jit. **The Future of Peacekeeping.** National Peace Institute. 1989.

Tessitore, John and Susan Woolfson. **Issues 45.** United Nations Association of U.S.A. 1991.

United Nations Publication. **The Blue Helmets.** 1989.

3. UN Arbitration, Mediation and Fact Finding -- Which Do We Need?

by Aram Fuchs

Arbitration, mediation and fact finding are essential aspects of solving disputes peacefully. The status quo situation of burdening the international institutions to develop ad hoc mechanisms to adjudicate disputes as they arise inherently produces a weak system. If dispute settlement institutions were created, with an air of permanence, it would add to chances of resolving disputes in a peaceful, mutually acceptable manner.

Which method of peaceful adjudication is the best? In this section, we will analyze each form available--arbitration, mediation and fact finding.

Submitting a dispute to an impartial third party, the essence of arbitration, is an ancient technique. Aristotle contrasted arbitration with judicial settlement in ancient Greece. During the Middle Ages in Italy, the Pope often served as an arbitrator, and later the monarchs of Europe arbitrated disputes outside their realms. King William I of the Netherlands, for instance, was invited to settle a river boundary question between the United States and Great Britain growing out of the Treaty of Ghent (1831). Even as recently as 1977 Queen Elizabeth II of the United Kingdom was asked to determine the boundary between Argentina and Chile in the Beagle Channel, and when war still threatened, the Pope finally resolved it.

Hague Peace Conference and the ICJ

During the late 19th Century, arbitration seemed to many internationalists to be a device that could be developed into a permanent institution to abolish war. This sentiment was one of the factors that brought about the First Hague Peace Conference in 1899, where the Permanent Court of Arbitration (actually a list of available qualified arbitrators plus a small bureau) was established. At the second Hague Peace Conference (1907), arbitration was again emphasized as a way of avoiding military conflict.

The mere availability of such a means of settlement, however, soon proved inadequate to cope with the forces at work in a world of sovereign states pursuing their own interests. The nations only used the international bodies when they could advance their own national interests. They ignored them if their rulings hurt their national prestige. Their intense national rivalries led to the carnage of the First World War.

A Permanent Court of International Justice was established as an outcome of the Paris Peace Conference ending World War I. The court's Statute provided for the compulsory adjudication of all international disputes (as in domestic disputes under national law) among members. But a country could easily avoid judgment by the court by simply not declaring themselves members. This happened all too frequently. The United States never joined.

After World War II, when the United Nations was established, the Court was renamed the International Court of Justice (ICJ) and its Statute was made an integral part of the UN Charter. Now all nations that are members of the UN are also parties to the Statute of the ICJ. But the number of nations agreeing to its compulsory jurisdiction is now only around 50, and most of these are hedged by reservations that make the World Court much less effective than it might otherwise be.

Arbitration a Possible Substitute

If the compulsory jurisdiction of the Court continues to prove unacceptable to the governments of the world, arbitration may be a substitute. Arbitration can produce binding, impartial and just decisions, but it is important to remember that its basis is mutual consent. Arbitration is "compulsory" or binding only in the sense that states agree beforehand to accept third-party settlement, in the expectation that the award will be fair and impartial. But it is up to the parties to the dispute to consent to all of the particulars of the arbitration. They must agree on the arbiters, the location and the setting of the trial. It is only then that they are obligated to abide by the arbiters' decision.

Arbitration's effectiveness depends on its larger context of political consensus within each state. In other words, if the parties do not wish to find the arbitration panel that is handing down the ruling legitimate then the rulings of the arbiters will never be considered binding. The push for an effective international government is presently caught in this bind.

The unobtrusive development of arbitration offers one hope for improving international dispute settlement in the foreseeable future. Arbitration is normally ad hoc, decentralized, and non-intrusive. Environmental treaties in particular lend themselves to peaceful dispute settlement mechanisms. A typical treaty is the International Convention Relating to Intervention on the High Seas in Cases of

Oil Pollution Casualties (1969), which provides for conciliation followed by arbitration. Another is the Convention on the International Maritime Satellite Organization (1976) which contains detailed arbitral provisions. A third is the Convention for the Protection of the Mediterranean Sea against Pollution (1976).

More recently, the Law of the Sea Convention (1982) adopted a complex dispute settlement mechanism. Its elaborate arbitral provisions were designed ingeniously to meet state demands for flexibility. The methods of dispute settlement are secondary to the idea that the parties agree to settle their disputes peacefully. Under the Law of the Sea Convention, parties in dispute are allowed complete freedom of choice with respect to the means of settlement. The four options are: (a) a new special Law of the Sea tribunal; (b) the present International Court of Justice; (c) a General Arbitral Tribunal; (d) a specific arbitral tribunal for certain categories of disputes. But if a party invokes reservations to the agreement that would make its execution impossible, then the parties are obliged to submit their dispute to the General Arbitral Tribunal. If two parties to a dispute have accepted different procedures for the settlement of disputes then they will be obligated to submit it to the General Arbitral Tribunal. It is interesting to note that while the Reagan Administration rejected the treaty, it did not raise any objections to the dispute settlement sections.

The Mediation Service Alternative

The embryonic international government called the United Nations must slowly attain the trust of the people of the world in order for its rulings eventually to be binding. One way to begin that trust is through non-binding mediation. Non-binding mediation will give the United Nations an opportunity to demonstrate its potential effectiveness to the national governments without obtaining a level of power, as in binding arbitration, that would be unacceptable to most national governments. An example is in the United States Federal Mediation and Conciliation Service. It has successfully mediated many thousands of labor-management disputes in the United States since 1947 and has generated interest in proposals for a permanent UN mediation and conciliation service.

The U.S. Mediation Service operates one national office in Washington, D.C., eight regional offices, and 72 field offices. With a staff of some 300 professional mediators, it handles over 28,000 joint and non-joint mediation cases a year and some 27,000 demands for arbitral panels (about 4,000 of which reach the award state). It has discretionary powers of inquiry and intervention and has developed the fine art of assisting parties in negotiation. The service is provided free at government expense. A system such as this on an international level could be the stepping stone to a stronger international dispute settlement system.

This method of solving disputes would allow nations that are hesitant to accept arbitration by an unknown agency to slowly gain trust in a similar type of institution. Both labor and management in the United States have grown increasingly accustomed to this cost-free government service provided to them. Today, mediators around the country find themselves accepted as helpmates of the collective bargaining process. There is no separate permanent institution in the international arena similar to the mediation machinery in the United States labor/management arena. Yet the stakes are infinitely higher.

There are no trained, full-time mediators employed in regional and field offices around the world. Most disputes are brought to the attention of the Security Council on an "ad hoc" basis. Under an "ad hoc" system, the United Nations is only able to react to a situation that will get even more tense by the time the Council is able to form an investigatory body to find out the facts. Even this action is subject to a veto by one of the permanent powers. The Security Council then appoints an agent, usually the Secretary General or one of his representatives, to attempt diplomatic intervention.

At times, the Security Council merely adopts a resolution urging a certain course of action and does not bother with the appointment of an agent. Sometimes the Security Council, unable to reach an agreement either because of a threatened or actual veto, does not act at all.

The Campaign for UN Reform has proposed the creation of a UN Regional Conciliation and Mediation Commission. It has suggested that regional offices be located on every continent and that the offices be staffed with trained professional mediators and conciliators familiar with the problems of each particular region.

The Fact-Finding Tool

Fact-finding is also an acceptable way to advance international cooperation. The UN Special Committee on the Charter and on the Strengthening of the Role of the Organization recognizes that just sending a fact-finding mission to a regional dispute demonstrates "the ability of the United Nations to maintain international peace and security" by "acquiring detailed knowledge about the factual circumstances of any dispute or conflict." Fact-finding is another tool frequently used in labor/management disputes to narrow the real issues in contention. Fact-finding can subdue the emotional fury that is usually intensified in a dispute between two sovereign states.

Many international disputes arise partly because of factual misunderstanding or disinformation. If the UN would establish a permanent team that would be able to establish the facts at the beginning of a dispute, it would tend to defuse the emotional aspects that often ignite a potential conflict. As long as states increase the use of any of the methods available to solve disputes peacefully, be it fact-finding, arbitration or mediation, the cause of peace will be advanced because the public will see that there is no dishonor in submitting a dispute to an impartial international body. There is only dishonor in leading one's people into a war that could have been avoided.

But as long as we have sovereign states willing to declare themselves above international law in order to pursue political prestige, the idea of binding arbitration will remain just a twinkle in every internationalist's eye. We need something that will prove to the people of the world that peaceful negotiations are the way to resolve their international disputes. It is the way to save the lives of their sons and now daughters, and a way to save them the cost of developing the latest killing machines. Considering that the compulsory settlement of disputes according to law in the courts is the very basis of domestic order, why do not national leaders and the public demand improvement of the World Court and the development of international law in order to build a truly just world order?

The way to convince the people of the world is to show success in non-binding mediation and fact-finding. The well-publicized peace conference in the mid-east is a start. While the conference is not under the authority of the United Nations, the UN may still be given a role in the ultimate settlement agreed upon. Conferences such as these could show the world that peaceful dispute settlement mechanisms are not only possible; they are necessary.

Discussion Questions

1. Do you believe nations should be able to choose the method of dispute settlement or should it be decided by an international authority?

2. Do you think the parties to a dispute should be required to submit their disputes to a form of arbitration under threat of global sanctions?

3. What body (military or political) should be available to enforce the decisions of an international judicial system?

4. How can the United Nations force nations into using an international dispute settlement system without violating their sovereignty?

5. How should UN dispute settlement mechanisms be funded?

REFERENCES AND SUGGESTED READINGS

Baratta, Joseph. **Monograph #7: International Arbitration: Improving its Role in Dispute Settlement.** Center for United Nations Reform Education, 1989.

Dinstein, Yoga. **War, Aggression and Self-Defence**, Grotius, 1988.

Hoffmann, Walter. **Monograph #2: Improving UN Dispute Settlement Machinery,** Center for United Nations Reform Education, 1984.

Rabow, Gerald, **Peace through Agreement: Replacing War with Non-Violent Dispute-Resolution Methods.** Praeger, 1990.

Sokol Colloquium (11th: 1990 University of Virginia School of Law), **Fact-Finding Before International Tribunals,** Transnational Publishers, 1991.

4. The World Court: How Do We Achieve Universal Acceptance?

by Gerald Biesecker-Mast

Among the many lessons to be learned from the Persian Gulf War is the necessity of strengthening the International Court of Justice (also known as World Court) so that it can peacefully arbitrate disputes of the kind which existed between Iraq and Kuwait prior to the war. Satish Kumar, chairman of the World Federalist Movement Council, put it this way in a recent issue of The Federalist Debate: "(Is it) not true that the whole international community is culpable for this avoidable disaster (the Gulf War) by not making the Court of Justice sufficiently strong and credible so that such territorial disputes could be subjected to judicial settlements?" In a new world order under law the international community must demand a World Court with broad enough jurisdiction and strong enough enforcement powers to settle disputes among nations and ensure the safety of all peoples.

Although it has gained higher visibility and experienced increased activity during recent years, the International Court of Justice is yet too weak to successfully serve the citizens of the world as an international arbiter of conflict among states. Yet, since its founding in 1920 as the Permanent Court of International Justice under the League of Nations many of the actions taken by the World Court have demonstrated the validity of the hope that one day nations will settle in court those matters for which they have so long relied on battlefields. In 1945, when it was reorganized under the United Nations and located at the Hague in the Netherlands, the International Court of Justice became an essential component of the present international security arrangement. Many of the cases upon which it has passed judgement or offered an advisory opinion exemplify the magnitude of possibility signified by the World Court. Others indicate serious flaws in its structure and scope of jurisdiction.

Perhaps a good example of the Court's success is the dispute between the U.S. and Canada over the marine boundary in the Gulf of Maine. In this case, both nations entered into a Special Agreement in 1981 asking that a special five-member chamber of the Court convene to determine the boundaries under question. The Chamber eventually decided to establish a new boundary line which divided the Gulf between the U.S. and Canada.

The Court's failures usually get more attention. For example, when the United States instituted proceedings against Iran in 1979 for seizing the U.S. embassy and holding its staff members as hostages, Iran refused to accept the Court's jurisdiction and rejected the Court's order that Iran restore the embassy, and release all U.S. hostages. That this case was eventually resolved only through a political agreement between the U.S. and Iran after months of harrowing experiences for U.S. diplomats demonstrates a primary weakness of the World Court system; namely, that it has no means to enforce its own rulings.

Furthermore, states' submission to the Court's jurisdiction is dependent on their consent, specified in treaties (such as the 1961 and 1963 Vienna Conventions to which both the United States and Iran were party), special agreements (such as the one entered into by the United States and Canada in the case just cited), and declarations by states recognizing compulsory jurisdiction. States which are parties to the Statute of the Court may at any time recognize the compulsory jurisdiction of the Court in relation to any other state accepting the same obligation.

The United States declared such a commitment in 1946; however, it included a reservation known as the Connolly amendment which excluded from the Court's jurisdiction "disputes with regard to matters which are essentially within the jurisdiction of the United States of America as determined by the United States of America." In other words, the United States gave itself the right to determine whether the Court had jurisdiction in any given case. Many critics like Thomas M. Franck believe that this amendment should have been repealed. According to Franck, "The hypocrisy of our 1946 acceptance lay in our decision to make the United States, rather than the Court, the judge of whether any case brought against us is 'essentially domestic' and so beyond the Court's purview. No court can be taken seriously if the defendants have the right to define its powers."

Nicaragua Decision

In any event, Franck's concern was rendered irrelevant when, in 1985, the United States declared World Court jurisdiction invalid for two years in anticipation of the case brought a day later against the United States by Nicaragua. At that time, Nicaragua accused the United States of violating international law, the United Nations charter, the Organization of American States charter, and other treaties by using American military force against Nicaragua, including the mining of Nicaraguan harbors. The Court determined that the case was legitimately within its jurisdiction and eventually ruled against the United States, deciding by a 12-3 majority that U.S. support of the contras was illegal, and further, by a 14-1 majority, that the U.S. mining of Nicaragua's harbors and its distribution of a CIA manual encouraging acts which oppose humanitarian principles also violated international law. When the U.S. refused to abide by the decision and used its veto to prevent any Security Council action against the United States, the World Federalist Association participated in a lawsuit against the administration for violating the judgement of the Court. But the case was dismissed when a district court judge in Washington D.C. ruled that the case fell outside his own jurisdiction since it was a political matter. During an appeal, the court held that the political exception doctrine did not apply but that the World Federalist Association lacked standing to sue.

Events like this work to undermine the credibility of the World Court and prevent nations from taking it seriously as a mechanism for settling disputes which might otherwise turn into violent confrontations. In response to the U.S. defiance of the World Court decision, Richard Bilder wrote:

"Scholars may argue at length whether the court's decision was right or wrong. But the judgement exists. It is legally binding and it won't go away. The

U.S. has a solemn legal obligation to respect the judgement, and our failure to do so will breach our treaty commitments under the U.N. Charter. Thus, the administration's stance raises very grave issues in terms of our national honor and reputation, our commitment to our treaties and the rule of law, and the future of international law and adjudication."

The United States never complied with any of the judgements rendered against it by the World Court in this case and vetoed all efforts to have the Security Council enforce the World Court's judgement. Meanwhile, each year until 1991, the General Assembly passed (sometimes by a vote of 91-2) a resolution calling for "full and complete compliance with the judgement" of the Court in the case of *Nicaragua vs. the United States*.

Other Issues Affecting Credibility

While a blatant refusal by a superpower to accept the decision of the World Court can do the most obvious damage to the Court's effectiveness, there are other issues which affect the Court's credibility. Prominent among these is the question of the Court's makeup. Article 9 of the Court's Statute maintains that "in the body as a whole the representation of the main forms of civilization and of the principal legal systems of the world should be assured." As Shabtai Rosenne (1989) has pointed out, however, "as a result of the process of decolonization, the earlier relatively clear distinction between the 'principal legal systems of the world' and the 'main forms of civilization' has become blurred." Because most previously colonized countries maintain the legal system introduced by the colonizers, more attention is being paid to the nationality of the candidate as a means of assuring fair representation of the world's political cultures on the Court.

If nations increasingly measure the Court's legitimacy in terms of the nationalities of the judges, the makeup of the Court will continue to dissatisfy many. This is difficult for the Court to address for at least two reasons. All of the members of the Court are elected for nine year terms by the UN General Assembly and the Security Council from a pool of nominees submitted by the members of the national groups in the Permanent Court of Arbitration. But an understanding has always existed that the five permanent members of the Security Council have the right to representation on the Court which leaves only 10 positions to constitute the rest of the World Court. Another difficulty associated with the creation of an inclusive court is the interpretation of the clause in Article 9 which states that "persons to be elected should individually possess the qualifications required." The qualifications it is possible to accumulate, whether judicial or academic, vary from country to country, and some nations may be excluded because their most respected jurists or legal academicians possess fewer credentials than those from wealthier nations. To mitigate these concerns, some have suggested that the number of seats on the World Court be expanded to permit a more inclusive membership. To do this would require amending the Statute, however, which is seen as unlikely since such an act would require formal ratification by all five permanent members of the Security Council. Nevertheless, some form of action is required because, as Rosenne puts it, "regardless of whether the composition of Court actually is a significant barrier for

some States to make use of its services, the fact remains that a number of States and noted authorities on international law continue to name this as a reason for the relative underutilization of the Court."

Perhaps the most neglected reason for the relative weakness of the World Court is the degree of popular ignorance concerning its function and authority. So long as nations can violate international obligations and treaties even after the World Court passes judgement against them without experiencing any protest from citizens who are committed to legal resolutions to international disputes, the Court will continue to exercise little power. Put differently, decisions of the court will need to be accessible to people before they will find the court's condemnation unacceptable. The lawsuit by World Federalists against the Reagan Administration's actions in Nicaragua is an example of one method of gaining public respect for the Court's activities and judgements.

Several recent developments should strengthen the Court's image and effectiveness. In 1989, the Secretary General announced the creation of a trust fund designed "to make available financial assistance to States where necessary so as to enable them to use the Court for the settlement of their legal differences". The General Assembly declared 1990-1999 the United Nations Decade of International Law "in order to advance the progressive development of international law and to encourage peaceful settlements to disputes." As part of the Decade, the General Assembly has suggested the "holding of a third international peace conference or other suitable conference at the end of the Decade." Also, by 1990, 50 states had accepted the "compulsory" jurisdiction of the Court, although many of them had attached reservations to their acceptance. Hopefully, acceptance of World Court jurisdiction is a trend that will continue.

Specific Policy Suggestions

What other constructive actions can be taken to strengthen the image and the functioning of the World Court? Taken from a number of sources, including World Federalist policy statements, here are some specific policy suggestions whose advocacy might contribute to the future health of the International Court of Justice.

1. Expand further the jurisdiction of World Court by lobbying U.N. constituents to declare their acceptance of its jurisdiction, without reservation. As more nations accept the compulsory jurisdiction of the Court, the effectiveness of its decisions will be determined less and less by the acceptance or rejection of its jurisdiction by specific nations for political purposes and more and more by universal recognition of its authority in matters of international law.

2. Encourage the United States to accept the compulsory jurisdiction of the Court. The Connolly amendment effectively gave the United States the authority to determine the jurisdiction of the World Court. In 1985, the U.S. abandoned any pretense of abiding by the compulsory jurisdiction of the court by arbitrarily declaring its relations with Central America off limits. When that was held to be ineffective by the World Court, President Reagan then formally revoked U.S. acceptance of the Court's compulsory jurisdiction. Nevertheless, there is a degree of confusion about the relation of the United States to the Court because the U.S. is still under the jurisdiction of the

Court in matters "pursuant to the United Nations Charter or treaties and conventions" (see Article 36 (1) of the UN Charter). Experts have identified as many as 70 treaties which require the U.S. to submit to the jurisdiction of the World Court. As a superpower which has historically identified itself with the principle of respect for the rule of law, the United States should set an example for other nations to follow by accepting the general jurisdiction of the Court without reservation.

3. Encourage the Security Council and General Assembly to request more advisory opinions from the Court. This would encourage even more court activity by giving it a chance to offer its opinion in cases involving international disputes not brought by states accepting the jurisdiction of the Court.

4. Make Court decisions available in all of the official United Nations languages. This is one way to encourage the broad distribution of the Court's opinions and hopefully to increase popular familiarity with the decisions and operations of the Court, hence decreasing the chances that nations can ignore the Court's judgements or opinions without experiencing some degree of embarrassment.

5. Educate primary and secondary school children in the workings of international law. This would be another way to increase the credibility of the Court by giving it a place in the consciousness of world citizens as a site of legitimate authority. Such programs would also help to foster a world cultural and political identity for the citizens of the world.

6. Support programs related to the Decade of International Law. The World Federalist Movement in conjunction with the World Network for International Law held an Experts' Roundtable on November 17,

1990 to discuss strategies for supporting the Decade. These experts encouraged the development of educational programs and media seminars for the purpose, drawing more public attention to the function and purpose of international legal structures. The Roundtable also called attention to the shortage of international law courses and professors in American educational institutions.

7. Establish a system of United Nations regional courts subordinate to the International Court of Justice. These regional courts would exist for the trial of individuals and private organizations accused of violating the U.N. charter or other laws and regulations which establish such courts as the arbiter of disputes. Appeals of decisions made by these regional courts might be heard by the International Court of Justice.

8. Amend the Charter to provide for the election of judges by the General Assembly alone. Among other things, this would put a stop to the current practice of giving five seats to the five permanent members of the Security Council. In general this would help promote a constitution of the court which more accurately reflects the configuration of the global population.

9. Amend the Charter to permit parties to a case in which one party refuses to comply to have recourse to the General Assembly for enforcement. This would strengthen the authority of the Court, particularly with respect to nations who currently enjoy the privilege of a veto on the Security Council. Presently, parties to a case theoretically only have recourse to the Security Council for enforcement.

Discussion Questions

1. Can the World Court with its present charter function as an effective arbiter of international conflict within a New World Order under Law?

2. How can nations be encouraged to accept the compulsory jurisdiction of the International Court of Justice?

3. What are ways to encourage the rule of international law without causing fear that national sovereignty is being surrendered?

4. As an educational organization, how can World Federalists encourage popular familiarity with the functions and activities of the International Court of Justice?

5. Would nations be more likely to refer their disputes to regional international courts than to the International Court of Justice?

6. Should the jurisdiction of the World Court be expanded to include international organizations and corporations?

REFERENCES AND SUGGESTED READINGS

Bilder, Richard. "In Contempt of Court." **St. Louis Post - Dispatch** (Aug. 7, 1986) 38.

Damrosch, Lori F. "An Overview of the World Court." **Transnational Perspectives** 15 (1989) 6-7.

Franck, Thomas M. "Let's Not Abandon the World Court." **New York Times** (July 17, 1986) I23.

Franck, Thomas M. **Judging the World Court.** New York: Priority Press, 1986.

Kumar, Satish. "The Gulf War and the World Order." **The Federalist Debate** 4 (1991) 5-6.

Rosenne, Shabtai. **The World Court: What It Is and How It Works.** Dordrecht: Martinus Nijhoff Publishers, 1989.

Tessitore, John, and Susan Woolfson. **Issues Before the 45th General Assembly of the United Nations.** Lexington: Lexington Books, 1991 (see pp. 214-220 on World Court).

5. An International Criminal Court: Should World Law Be Applied to Individuals?

by Bryan F. MacPherson

The traditional subjects of international law are nations and not individuals. Consequently, it has been nations, not national leaders or other individuals, that have generally been bound by international law and held responsible for its violation. Thus, while international law may hold a nation liable to pay reparations if it engages in aggression, the national leaders who directed that aggression have usually been beyond the scope of international law. Punishment for crimes having international consequences, if any, depends largely upon the application of national law. This limitation on the reach of international law is reflected in the jurisdiction of the International Court of Justice, which is commonly referred to as the World Court. Only nations can be parties to cases before the World Court——individuals can neither initiate cases nor be defendants.

The Nuremberg Precedent

Today, however, most nations and international lawyers recognize that there are circumstances, albeit limited, under which individuals should be held accountable for violations of international law. This acceptance of international jurisdiction over individuals grew largely out of the aftermath of the suffering and destruction wrought by World War II. The trials of national and military leaders that were conducted at Nuremberg and Tokyo established the principle that individuals may under some circumstances be held personally accountable for violations of international law. Nonetheless, the conduct for which the accused were convicted——war crimes, crimes against peace, and crimes against humanity——had not been expressly made "criminal" by then existing international instruments. As a result, the Nuremberg and Tokyo tribunals have been criticized as applying *ex post facto* laws.

This criticism would not be as applicable today. Nuremberg established the precedent that leaders of governments could be held individually accountable for unjustified aggression. In 1949, the international community also adopted the Geneva Conventions dealing with the conduct of war. Most nations are parties to these conventions which specify the type of conduct that may constitute war crimes for which individuals can be held personally

The Nuremberg Trials -- Nazi leaders include (front row): Goring (extreme left), Hess (second from left), Ribbentrop (third from left), and Schacht (extreme right). Radio Times Hulton Picture Library.

responsible. Genocide was made a punishable crime by the Genocide Convention which the UN adopted in 1948. Subsequently, a number of additional international conventions have been adopted by the world community dealing with other international crimes. Among the conduct covered by these conventions is apartheid, hijacking and other crimes involving aircraft, crimes against diplomats, taking of hostages, and narcotics trafficking. We can only speculate on what additional crimes will be recognized by the world community in the future. One commentator, M. Cherif

Bassiouni, suggests that a wide variety of international offenses, including destruction or theft of national treasures, causing harm to the environment, violating human rights, trafficking in obscene materials, and bribery of foreign officials, could eventually become the subject of international criminal law.

Ad Hoc War Crimes Trials Open to Criticism

There is currently no international court with jurisdiction to try these international crimes; they must be enforced by existing national courts. With respect to war crimes, a nation may prosecute crimes committed by its own forces in its own established courts (including courts martial) and may try opposing forces, if it is able to apprehend them, in these same courts. Alternatively, *ad hoc* tribunals, such as the Nuremberg and Tokyo tribunals, may be used to try war criminals. This system is subject to a number of criticisms. Enforcement by a state against its own forces will be effective only if the state has the will to comply with the laws of war. Where violation of those laws is consistent with government policy, the state cannot be expected to prosecute its nationals for war crimes. Moreover, the emotions that are present in wartime situations may lead a state to excuse violations committed by its nationals or to view them as less serious than similar offenses committed by the enemy.

The use of *ad hoc* tribunals to try opposing forces is also unsatisfactory. The Nuremberg and Tokyo tribunals, while establishing the principle that individuals may be held criminally liable for violating the laws of war, have been criticized by some for alleged bias, prejudgment of guilt, and denial of due process. A serious deficiency with such tribunals is that generally all the judges are selected from the victorious states, while only those on the defeated side of the conflict are brought to trial. Thus, unless states are vigorous in prosecuting members of their own forces who violate the laws of war, only those on the losing side will be prosecuted. Irrespective of the merit to these criticisms of the Nuremberg and Tokyo tribunals, the procedures followed gave the appearance of unfairness. If the rule of law is to gain acceptance by the international community, it is not enough that justice be done, but what is done must also appear to be just. Trial of war criminals by a truly unbiased international tribunal will remedy these deficiencies in the existing system.

Prosecution of the other international and transnational crimes referred to above, must also be in a national court. If the perpetrator of a crime flees to another country, the country where the crime was committed must obtain his extradition in order to try him. Alternatively, the accused may be tried in the country in which he is located if that country has extended its criminal jurisdiction over crimes committed outside its territory. The international conventions dealing with criminal activities referred to above require the parties to establish their jurisdiction over the specified crimes, even under circumstances where the crime was not committed within the country. For example, a convention might require nations to extend their jurisdiction to instances where the state or its national was the victim of the crime, or where the accused is a national of the state. In addition, the conventions typically require the country where the accused is found to treat the offense as an extraditable offense, and if it is unable under its laws to extradite

the offender, the country must try him in its own courts.

Extradition Problems

Although this system of criminal law enforcement works well in most cases, it occasionally breaks down. This is most often the case with politically motivated crimes, such as terrorism, and with major narcotics trafficking where the traffickers have substantial money and power. Extradition is generally available only if there is an extradition treaty between the state where the accused is found and the requesting state, and the accused may escape punishment where there is no treaty. Even where there is an extradition treaty, there is no guarantee that the accused will be brought to trial. Most states recognize the political offense exception to extradition. The exception is intended to avoid taking sides in the internal affairs of the requesting state, both out of a belief that it should not interfere in the political affairs of another state and out of a concern that the political offender may someday come into power. It is also grounded in the concern that a political offender may not receive a fair trial from the courts of the requesting state, and if convicted will receive an unreasonably harsh sentence. Finally, there exists the belief that political dissent, and even rebellion, may be legitimate——the distinction between a terrorist and a freedom fighter is often not clear. An attempt to try the Kaiser following World War I was unsuccessful when the Netherlands declined to extradite him because of the political nature of his alleged crimes.

Many states will also not extradite their own citizens. This exception, like the political offense exception, is based in part upon the concern that their citizens might not receive fair treatment in the courts of foreign states, either because other states may not ensure due process or because they might be prejudiced against foreigners. It is also grounded in nationalistic feelings to the effect that it is inappropriate to hand over their citizens for trial by a foreign state.

Too frequently, these exceptions prevent the effective prosecution of transnational criminals. The political offense exception often frustrates efforts to extradite the political terrorists. Terrorists usually seek refuge in states where either the government or a significant portion of the population is sympathetic to their cause. Consequently, even if a convention requires the state in which the offender has taken refuge to try the offender if it does not extradite him, the state may lack the political will or the jurisdiction under its domestic law to prosecute the offender.

Terrorist Intimidation

Terrorist groups have also used intimidation to coerce states to release members who have been captured. Abul Abbas, the hijacker of the Achille Lauro, is an example. He was released by Italy, and subsequently both Egypt and Yugoslavia allowed him to escape prosecution. There have been many instances of coercion being employed to secure the release of terrorists. The case of Mohammed Hamadei, who in 1985 hijacked TWA flight 847 and killed an American in the process, is another example. The United States sought his extradition after he was apprehended in Germany. Terrorists kidnapped two German businessmen in an effort to block his extradition and obtain his release. These efforts were only partially successful——Germany declined extradition but tried him itself, resulting in a life sentence. The German businessmen, however, remain hostages.

As a result, terrorists too often escape punishment and are able to continue their activities. According to the CIA, there were 1,152 terrorist incidents between 1968 and 1976, including 391 involving U.S. citizens or property. According to State Department records, only about 20 percent of international kidnappings are punished. Between 1970 and 1975, only 267 individuals involved in international terrorism were apprehended. Of these, 58 secured safe conduct to another country, 16 were released upon the demand of other terrorists, and another 39 were freed without punishment.

The situation in Columbia is another disappointing example. There, the judiciary and the political system have become intimidated by drug traffickers and political terrorists. For a time, the government extradited drug traffickers for trial in the United States. However, extradition to the United States was unpopular and is no longer politically feasible. As a result, Columbia will prosecute drug traffickers in its own courts. This is not likely to lead to satisfactory results. Columbia's conviction rate for such criminals has been quite low. Moreover, even if convicted, drug barons such as Escobar are likely to receive relatively light sentences to be served under pleasant conditions. There is speculation that Escobar may be able to continue to run his drug empire from his prison cell.

As a result of these deficiencies in the existing international enforcement system, the deterrent value of criminal law is lessened, because criminals and potential criminals expect to be able to avoid responsibility for their actions.

Sophisticated terrorists understand how to manipulate the system by seeking refuge in states that are unlikely to either extradite or prosecute them. They therefore believe that they can commit their crimes with impunity. Another danger is that states which are unable to obtain extradition of the alleged offender may resort to self-help, such as the abduction by Israel of Adolph Eichman from Argentina, and the seizure of Noriega by the United States. While self-help may bring criminals to justice, it does so at considerable cost to the world order. Self-help endangers lives and violates the sovereignty of independent states, thereby increasing international tensions. It also may harm the standing in the world community of states employing it.

Recent Advances

Recent increases in worldwide terrorism, drug trafficking, and the Gulf War have caused many in the international community to question the adequacy of these existing methods of dealing with transnational criminality. In 1988, Prime Minister Robinson of the Republic of Trinidad and Tobago called for greater international cooperation to control international crime and for creation of an international criminal court ("ICC"). Many other states have recognized that an ICC could be a useful tool for combating international crime. In 1990, the U.S. Congress included a provision in the Foreign Operations Appropriations Act requiring the President to explore the need for an ICC and to report the results of his efforts to Congress. In July 1991, the World Federalist Association (WFA) submitted a report to the Department of State outlining its proposals for an international court.

The idea of an international court to try crimes that are international in scope is not new. One of the first efforts to establish a truly international court to try international offenses was a 1938 Terrorism Convention that never received enough support to come into force. The UN International Law Commission proposed a draft statute for an ICC in 1951 and revised in 1953 that accompanied draft Codes of Offenses against the Peace and Security of Mankind. The draft codes dealt primarily with major Nuremberg-type crimes. The International Law Commission continues to study the matter, and in 1990, it issued a report on the prospects for an international court which pointed out many of the issues that will have to be addressed. The U.N. Human Rights Commission endorsed a proposal for a court to try individuals accused of the crime of apartheid in 1980. Other proposals have included reports of the ABA's Section of International Law, recommending in 1978 an ICC to try offenses against diplomats and civil aviation, and in 1990 a court to try narcotics traffickers.

An ICC would not be a panacea that would cure all of the problems associated with the international enforcement of criminal laws. There would continue to be difficulties in obtaining custody of alleged offenders, especially if they are the high government officials like Saddam Hussein and Noriega. Nonetheless, the WFA believes that an international court would make a considerable contribution to more effective law enforcement. An ICC would provide a fair, unbiased tribunal to try international criminals in which all states could have confidence.

Those accused of war crimes would be assured of a fair trial by a court that was not composed exclusively of representatives of the opposing states, and the law could be applied equally to both the victorious and the vanquished forces. With respect to other crimes, states could have confidence that the court would treat politically motivated criminals fairly, and that any punishment meted out was for the accused's conduct, not for his political beliefs. The multi-national character of the court should assure states that their citizens will receive fair trials, unbiased by any prejudices that might exist in the courts of a foreign state. Finally, an international court will be less likely to be subject to political influence or intimidation than would any national court. Consequently, aggrieved states could have confidence that guilty parties will not receive unduly lenient treatment, as might result if the offender were tried in the court of a state sympathetic to his cause, or otherwise reluctant to try the offender. An ICC that is structured to ensure fairness would largely remove the bases underlying the exceptions to extradition for political offenses and a state's own nationals. States consequently would have no reason to apply the exceptions to cases before the ICC. It should therefore enhance the deterrent to international crimes by increasing the likelihood that international criminals are prosecuted, convicted, and punished.

Obstacles to be Overcome

It will not be easy to obtain sufficient consensus from the international community in order to make an ICC a reality. Although many states support the concept of an international court, other states are opposed to the idea. Moreover, it may be difficult of obtain agreement on the specific details for such a court. Much of the resistance to the idea of an ICC comes from

mere inertia and the reluctance of states to try something new. However there are some very real concerns that will have to be addressed. Among these is the concern that an international court will become politicized. This could result in the court interpreting crimes in a manner that would release some criminals who could no longer be prosecuted, or in the court entertaining frivolous prosecutions of a state's citizens or national leaders. In addition, the world has many different legal systems with different views of how criminal law should be enforced, and it will be necessary to achieve agreement on structure of the court and the procedures that will be applied. A number of states are also concerned with whether an international court will be cost effective or will detract from other methods of combating international crime. The WFA believes that these and other potential difficulties can be overcome. The highlights of the WFA's proposal are summarized below.

The WFA believes that an ICC should be affiliated with the UN. It would be ideal if it was an organ of the UN. However, this would require amending the UN Charter, which would be difficult to achieve. A more realistic approach would be for it to be created as a subsidiary organ of the Security Council, as that would only require approval of the Security Council. Alternatively, an ICC could be an independent agency of the UN created by a separate convention. The WFA proposal does not recommend that the jurisdiction of the World Court be expanded to include criminal matters, since that would detract from its current work. The WFA suggests that the judges of an ICC should be nominated by state bar associations and elected by a vote of both the General Assembly and the Security Council (without the veto applying). This is comparable to the election method used for the World Court.

WFA's Proposal

Past proposals for an ICC have run the gamut from jurisdiction over a few related offenses to jurisdiction over a wide variety of offenses. WFA believes that ultimately there should be an ICC that will have broad jurisdiction over a wide range of international crimes, but many states may be reluctant at this time to surrender their criminal jurisdiction to an unproven international tribunal. Accordingly, the WFA proposes that, initially, the ICC have jurisdiction over war crimes and the crimes specified in the conventions pertaining to genocide, hijacking and other crimes against civil aviation, taking of hostages, crimes against diplomats, and narcotics trafficking. Only jurisdiction over war crimes would be specified in the statute of the court. Jurisdiction over the other offenses would be conferred by separate protocols that would be opened for signature at or shortly after the time that the statute of the court is signed. Other international crimes could be added later by separate protocols. By limiting the scope of an ICC's initial jurisdiction, the international community will hopefully be willing to give an ICC a try.

Except for major war crimes and mass genocide, jurisdiction of the ICC would be concurrent with the existing jurisdiction of national courts. Under the conventions dealing with these international crimes, the states in which the accused is found are required to either extradite the accused or to try him in its own national courts. Granting an ICC concurrent

jurisdiction over these offenses would interfere little with the existing enforcement system, since it merely gives the state having custody an additional alternative to trying or extraditing the accused. The state seeking prosecution of the accused would not be likely to object to trial by an ICC, as it is unlikely that trial by an ICC will lead to more lenient treatment than trial by a reluctant state.

With respect to war crimes, WFA proposes that states be permitted to prosecute their own nationals and nationals of the opposing side that are charged with only minor war crimes, in either its own courts or in the ICC. If, however, a state wished to try an individual from the opposing side for a "major" war crime, it would have to bring the case before the ICC. A war crime would be "major" if a sentence greater than a specified minimum was sought. By granting exclusive jurisdiction over major war crimes to an international tribunal, those facing a substantial penalty will be ensured a fair and unbiased trial. Similarly, the WFA proposes that the ICC have exclusive jurisdiction over mass genocide, but concurrent jurisdiction over lesser acts of genocide.

Most prior proposals for an ICC have specified the number of judges, and have assumed that trials would be by the full court. Trial by the full court would be appropriate if the court were conducting only a few Nuremberg-type trials a year, but would be unworkable if the court were trying hundreds of common drug trafficking cases a year. Moreover, specifying the number of judges in the court statute would be too rigid and would not allow for growth of the court. WFA recommends that the court be composed of between nine and 15 judges (no two from the same state) with the number to be determined by the participating states at the time of voting based upon the court's workload. Trials should be conducted by a panel of three judges, with unanimity required for verdicts and appeals going to the full court. If the court's workload justifies, additional "associate" judges could be elected who would act as trial judges but would not hear appeals.

Due Process to be Assured

There should be no dispute that trials by an ICC should meet international standards of due process as set forth in applicable international instruments. This would assure defendants of rights comparable to those of defendants in US courts. Disagreements as to the specific procedures that should be followed by the court will have to be resolved in view of the varied legal systems in the world. For example, states that derive their legal systems from English common law generally provide for trials by jury and for prosecution by a state representative. In contrast, civil law countries generally have no jury trials and the prosecution is conducted by an unbiased judiciary. The WFA proposes that the ICC not use jury trials and that representatives of the aggrieved states conduct the prosecutions, except in cases of major war crimes or mass genocide where the prosecutor would be appointed by the Security Council. The purpose of an independent prosecutor in civil law systems is to ensure that the accused is not harassed by meritless proceedings, but this goal can be accomplished as well by providing a preliminary hearing before a court panel that can dismiss frivolous cases.

Some proposals for an ICC have included a separate board of probation and parole and separate international penal facilities. The WFA proposal agrees that provision should be made for probation or parole, but it believes that authority for them should be vested in the court itself. The WFA also does not believe that an international penal facility is appropriate at this time, and that it would constitute an unnecessary expense. Instead, WFA believes that existing state penal facilities should be utilized. The court might, for example, wish to confine a prisoner in a facility near his home. Also, a state extraditing its citizen for trial before the court might insist upon him being imprisoned within that state.

In sum, the current system of prosecuting and punishing international crime has been insufficient to deal with many serious crimes, particularly war crimes and genocide, but also including drug trafficking and political terrorism. Too often major international criminals are able to avoid responsibility for their actions because of inadequacies in the current extradition system, and trials of war criminals conducted by tribunals of the opposing side often give the appearance of unfairness.

The WFA believes that an ICC would be a valuable adjunct in the fight against international crime and would be a major building block in any future world federation. By providing a clearly unbiased alternative to domestic courts, the reluctance of states to extradite their own nationals or persons accused of political crimes should be lessened. The court should, therefore, ensure that a greater number of international criminals are held accountable. An ICC would represent a powerful symbol of the community of nations' commitment to a world order that is based upon the rule of law. It would illustrate the belief that international crimes are crimes against all peoples, and it would reflect the determination that international criminals be held accountable for their actions.

Discussion Questions:

1. Do you believe that an international court to try individuals accused of international crimes would serve a valuable purpose? If so, what crimes would be appropriate for international trials?

2. Under what circumstances would it be reasonable to try national leaders, including American presidents, before an International Criminal Court? How would the court obtain custody of national leaders?

3. How would you organize and structure an international criminal court? What should be its relationship to the World Court and the UN? How would it be funded?

4. Should the sentences imposed by an international court be based upon the law of the state in which the crime was committed, the law of some other interested state, or upon a world standard? If based upon a world standard, how would it be determined?

5. Would the creation of a special international criminal court be an important step toward a world federal government?

REFERENCES AND SUGGESTED READINGS

Anderson. "An International Criminal Court——An Emerging Idea" 15 **NOVA L. Rev.** 433 (1991).

Bassiouni. "A Comprehensive Strategic Approach on International Cooperation for the Prevention, Control & Suppression of International & Transnational Criminality" 15 **NOVA L. Rev.** 353 (1991).

Comment. "The Political Offense Exception: A Historical Analysis and Model for the Future" 64 **Tulane L.R.** 1195 (1990).

B. Ferencz. **An International Criminal Court——A Step Toward World Peace.** (1980) (2 vols.).

Scharf. "The Jury is Still Out on the Need for an International Criminal Court" **Duke J. Comp. & Int'l L.** (Summer 1991).

Part Two
BUILDING THE INSTITUTIONS FOR GLOBAL GOVERNANCE

6. Should There Be a Global Parliament? What Is the Binding Triad?

by Richard Hudson

The heart of any human institution -- whether it be the family, the city, the state, the nation, or a world organization -- is its decision-making system. Is it just? Is it rational? Is it compassionate? Does it work?

On the global level today, it must be stated that the decision-making system is not just, not rational, not compassionate, and does not work.

The United Nations is the core of the global decision-making system. The world organization has done, and is doing, much good work. However, measured against the awesome and urgent needs of the planet Earth, the UN system is failing to meet the challenges of our times.

The case was well put in the path-breaking Stockholm Initiative on Global Security and Governance: "Common Responsibility in the 1990's" (April 22, 1991). The 48-page report, signed by 36 world leaders including Willy Brandt, Norwegian Prime Minister Gro Harlem Brundtland, Swedish Prime Minister Ingvar Carlsson, Jimmy Carter, Czech and Slovak President Vaclav Havel, Robert MacNamara, Julius Nyerere, Eduard Shevardnadze, and Maurice Strong made these declarations in the preface to the Stockholm Initiative:

-- "Securing peace, sustainable development and democracy requires nations, in their common interest, to create a new system of global security and governance.

-- Increasing economic and ecological interdependencies have not been met by a corresponding strengthening of global cooperation and governance.

-- We need a new world order, based on justice and peace, democracy and development, human rights and international law."

The Stockholm Initiative makes 28 proposals, the last two of which read as follows:

(27) "That a World Summit on Global Governance be called, similar to the meetings in San Francisco and Bretton Woods in the 1940's." (28) "As a matter of priority, the establishment of an independent International Commission on Global Governance."

The Stockholm drafters were wise to include this admonition: "We believe that the best form of preparation for such a summit would be the work of an independent commission, non-governmental in the nature of the Commissions whose work we have referred to in this memorandum." (These other commissions were the Brandt North-South Commission, the Olof Palme Commission on Disarmament and Security, the Brundtland Commission on Environment and Development, and the Nyerere South Commission.)

Inconsistencies in the Stockholm Initiative

The first proposal of the recommendations under "Global Governance," No. 21, must, I believe, be questioned:

"That the United Nations takes on a broadened mandate at the Security Council level, following the wider understanding of security which has developed, and that its composition and the use of the veto be reviewed."

It strikes me that this proposal flies in the face of another observation of the Stockholm Initiative:

"Decisions on most crucial issues are taken outside of these (UN) organizations by a small group of countries. Summits and meetings of the Group of Seven (G7) or even smaller constellations have become the focus of attention, rather than the top level meetings of international organizations.

"Such an order of global leadership will not only be increasingly unacceptable to the more than 150 other nations of the world. It will also be increasingly ineffective. When interdependencies have grown to such a degree as they have, global security, economic stability and sustainable development can only be achieved by the active participation of all parts of the world."

There is no mention in the Stockholm Initiative of the contradiction between its suggestion of expanded powers of the UN Security Council, essentially an undemocratic body, and its recommendation

that global decisions "be achieved by the active participation of all parts of the world." Nor is there any mention of empowering the UN General Assembly, representing by far the closest approach to a global decision-making body, with legislative authority, nor of changing its voting system to accord more nearly with current political realities.

In seeking to work toward a just and effective system of global security and governance, we must build on what we have achieved, which is considerable, but we must not be satisfied with half-measures, such as tinkering around with the Security Council or the Economic and Social Council. On the other hand, we must be wary of grandiose plans to dump the United Nations Charter and start all over again to draft a new world constitution. (Analogies to the American experience in Philadelphia in 1787 are not valid; the UN Charter is a much better and more developed document than the Articles of Confederation.)

The United Nations today has, in incipient form, three of the four essential attributes of a rational system of global governance:

(1) An executive department headed by a Secretary-General chosen by a method that is not perfect but that nevertheless reflects current world politics fairly well. (The UN Charter provides: "The Secretary-General shall be appointed by the General Assembly upon the recommendation of the Security Council.")

(2) A judicial system in the form of the International Court of Justice (World Court) that is being used increasingly and that can be expanded to meet growing world needs to settle justiciable issues.

(3) An enforcement system that includes economic and political sanctions, fact-finding and peacekeeping missions, and,

ultimately, military force.

A World Parliament: The Missing Element

The missing fourth attribute of a rational system of global governance is a world parliament, or legislature.

UN General Assembly Plenary Session, September 1990. UN photo 176105.

The UN General Assembly, with its absurd one nation, one vote decision-making system, and its authority to make only non-binding recommendations, has no chance to make global laws. This has caused the international community to repeatedly go outside the General Assembly in efforts to solve all manner of global problems through new treaties and conventions. A prime example of this approach was the global effort to achieve a Law of the Sea (LOS) treaty. The work began in 1967 with the historic address in the UN of Ambassador Arvid Pardo of Malta in which he called for the oceans beyond the limits of national jurisdiction to be made "the common heritage of mankind." After 15 years, in 1982, a treaty was achieved, but now, nine years later, only 47 of the 60 necessary ratifications have been acquired. Furthermore, some of us who were deeply involved in the process feel that even if the LOS treaty were in effect today, it wouldn't make much difference. The LOS treaty does not represent a major advance toward the effective governance of the 71 percent of

the surface of the Earth covered by oceans; for the most part, it leaves control of the seas to the sovereign nation-states. Worse, it now seems to me that the international community is going to make the same mistake again in trying to cope with environmental issues.

There is a way out of this impasse: The Binding Triad system for global decision-making. By making amendments to only two articles to the United Nations Charter, the General Assembly could be transformed into a functioning global legislature able to pass politically balanced and enforceable laws.

Two Charter Amendments Required

The first amendment would be to Article 18, and would change the decision-making from one nation, one vote to a weighted voting system based on three factors: (1) one nation, one vote (the same as now), (2) population, and (3) contributions to the regular UN budget (which are a rough measure of GNP). In order for a resolution to pass (and become global law), it would need to be approved be a certain majority on all three "legs." This majority percentage would be higher than 50 percent and lower than 67 percent, and very likely the final figure cannot be reached until the tough negotiations preceding the end of process. Another closely related factor would be the scale of assessments on the third leg, since the present scale would clearly have to be revised before the two Binding Triad amendments could enter into force. There is virtual consensus in the UN that the current U.S. contribution of 25 percent to the regular budget is too high, and would give the U.S. too much influence on the third leg. Perhaps a maximum contribution of 15 percent from any one nation might be about right.

The second amendment for the Binding Triad system would be to Article 13, which would change resolutions of the UN General Assembly from being recommendations into being binding and enforceable global laws. These laws could be enforced by economic and political sanctions and/or fact-finding and peacekeeping operations. However, the General Assembly would not have at its disposal the use of military force, which would remain the prerogative of the Security Council. The rationale on this is that military force as a political tool is historically on its way out. The ultimate objective of the Binding Triad system is to eliminate the system of war by replacing it with a system of peace based on global law. (What a pity that sanctions could not have been applied longer in the Persian Gulf crisis, not only to have avoided the war but also to have demonstrated that in the long run they do work.)

The Democratization Issue

Before approaching the critical question of the strategy of how to bring the Binding Triad system into being, let me address the issue of the democratization of the global system, which often comes up. I argue that the Binding Triad makes the maximum possible mutation toward world democracy within the time frame open to us to start solving urgent global problems. I argue further that the best way to promote democracy around the world is within nations; witness what has happened in the absolute monarchy of Nepal and despotism of General Stroessner in Paraguay.

Notions of American style democracy on a world level at this period of history, are, in my view, naive. Holding elections on a global level would take much too long, and the practical implications are overwhelming. Americans, in particular, tend to forget that we have been working on this great experiment for more than 200 years. In the beginning, you were free to vote -- if you were white, male, and owned property. Most Americans forget that for the first 124 years of our government -- from 1789 to 1913 -- U.S. Senators were not popularly elected but were appointed by the state governments, much in the same manner as national governments now appoint their representative to the UN. I say: Let's get a global legislature now, even though it's not perfect. We have a lot of pressing business to do.

So, how to do it?

The technicalities are not difficult. Article 108 of the UN Charter reads:

"Amendments to the present Charter shall come into force for all Members of the United Nations when they have been adopted by a vote of two thirds of the members of the General Assembly and ratified in accordance with their respective constitutional processes by two thirds of the Members of the United Nations, including all the permanent members of the Security Council."

Forget Article 109, which provides for the calling of "A General Conference of the Members of the United Nations for the purpose of reviewing the present Charter." The UN Charter has been revised substantively twice without a "general conference," once to increase the number of Security Council members from 11 to 15 and once to double the membership of Economic and Social Council.

The practical question is whether global-minded people can rally political support for a specific proposal, namely, the Binding Triad system, or whether, as in past decades, we will let a hundred, or a thousand, flowers bloom. I think the time has come to choose.

Discussion Questions

1. Can the world rely on the present treaty and convention-making system to solve world problems?

2. Should the UN system be accepted more or less as it is, or should it be dumped and a totally new start be made on global governance?

3. Is the Binding Triad proposal within the realm of acceptance before the year 2000?

4. What practical steps can be taken to advance the Binding Triad proposal?

SUGGESTED READINGS

Newcombe, Hanna. **Design for a Better World.** University Press of America: Lanham, MD, 1983.

Make the United Nations Work: The Case for the Binding Triad. 20 minute video produced by Center for War/Peace Studies, 218 East 18 Street, New York, NY 10003.

The World Needs a Way to Make Up its Mind: The Binding Triad. Center for War/Peace Studies.

7. Should There Be a UN Parliamentary Assembly and/or Direct Popular Election of UN Delegates?

by Ron Glossop

In many ways the UN is a school for democracy for the whole world. The rules set down in the Charter as well as those adopted by the organization later apply equally to all representatives and all nations. All national governments are treated as equals in that each can have five representatives and one vote in the General Assembly. Different points of view can be openly expressed in debate, and even those who disagree must quietly listen. Issues are decided by majority vote. Committees are formed to promote collective decision-making on problems to be addressed, and the work of the committees is done in a democratic way, even including the publication of minority reports. Officers are elected as are the representatives to the various organs of the UN, such as the members of the Economic and Social Council and the non-permanent members of the Security Council.

But it is not difficult to find aspects of the UN which could be more democratic. For example, each country in the UN gets one vote in the General Assembly regardless of its population. A country like India with a population of 832 million people has the same voting power as a country like the Bahamas with a population of less than 250,000. Five countries (U.S., U.S.S.R., Britain, China, and France) are permanent members of the Security Council with a veto power, while other countries are elected for two-year terms, with 156 countries vying for 10 seats on the Council. Furthermore, none of the national representatives at the UN are elected; all are appointed by their national governments. Even though the Charter of the UN starts out with the words, "We the peoples of the United Nations," the fact is that the UN is an organization for the national governments rather than for the people.

How might the UN be made more democratic? One way might be to change the UN itself, but that is not easy to do, especially if it requires a change in the Charter. The Charter can be amended (in fact, the size of the Security Council has been increased from 11 members originally to 15 now, and the size of the Economic and Social Council has been increased twice, from an original 18 to 27 to 54), but proposed amendments are subject to the veto of the permanent members.

A Second Assembly Under Article 22

Could the UN be made more democratic without changing the Charter? One

provision of the Charter has been viewed as a vehicle for such change. Article 22 says: "The General Assembly may establish such subsidiary organs as it deems necessary for the performance of its functions." One proposal with several variations is that the General Assembly could call for the creation of a "Second Assembly" to act as an advisory body. Four possibilities have been set forth by the International Network for a UN Second Assembly (INFUSA), an organization led by Jeffrey J. Segall of London, U.K. (1) The members of the Second Assembly could be directly elected by the usual voting population. (2) The members of the Second Assembly could be directly elected by voters who have specifically registered for voting in this election. (3) The members of the Second Assembly could be elected by members of a special electoral college consisting of representatives of non-governmental organizations and institutions. (4) The members of the Second Assembly could be selected by a commission of representatives of non-governmental organizations and institutions.

A fifth variation on this theme is being supported by the World Federalist Movement, 777 UN Plaza, 12th Floor, New York, NY 10017, with Dieter Heinrich being the main spokesperson. According to this view, the Second Assembly should be composed of parliamentarians from national parliaments or persons selected by them. The principle here is that the persons at the UN would be selected by the legislative branch of governments rather than by the executive branch, and thus supposedly would be closer to the electorate.

One problem for all of these proposals is to determine not only how many total representatives there will be in this Second Assembly but even more important, what system of representation will be used. Will the number of representatives be based on the population (in which case China would have 22% of all the representatives and India would have 16%, while the Soviet Union would have 6% and the U.S. would have 5%)? Or should the number of representatives be based on the square root of the population with each country having at least one, so that larger countries would not have so many more representatives than smaller countries? Or should there be some system which tries to combine population and "power" in determining the number of representatives?

The Clark-Sohn Proposal

One fairly well known effort to do this kind of combination formula is that produced by Grenville Clark and Louis Sohn in their book World Peace Through World Law. According to their system the four most populous nations (China, India, Soviet Union, and the U.S.) would each have 30 votes, the next 10 populous countries would have 12 votes each, the next 15 would have 8 votes each, the next 20 would have 6 votes each, the next 30 would have 4 votes each, the next 40 would have 3 votes each, and the others would have one vote each. In the more populous groupings there would be less developed countries at the top of the grouping and more developed ones at the bottom, so population would be somewhat balanced by economic power, but it would never be the case that a less populous country would have more votes than a more populous one.

The actual listing by Clark and Sohn of how many votes particular countries would get has gone through shifts with the passage of time, indicating that the application of this approach at any one time is ad hoc even though the general approach stays the same. This fact raises the question of how the number of votes would be calculated with the passage of time. What would happen, for example, if the Soviet Union breaks up into several republics? How many votes would each have? There is no automatic calculation which would determine the answer. It is doubtful that such an ad hoc system for deciding specifically how many votes a given country would have would be acceptable. A system based on the square root of the population would be much less debatable. But even then one faces the paradoxical situation that a country which breaks up into many separate nation-states will gain votes in the process while the union of countries such as may occur in the European Community would mean a loss of votes in the world parliament. Of course, that is also the case with the present one-vote-per-nation system in the General Assembly.

The problem of representation in a parliament based on population might be approached on a regional basis rather than a national basis. With such a plan there would be a given number of votes for South America, a given number for North America, a given number for Africa, and so on, based on population. What may be surprising is that on this basis Asia would have 60% of the votes, Europe would have 13%, Africa would have 12.5%, North America would have 8%, South America would have 5.5%, and Oceania would have .5%. To put it in other terms that may be somewhat disconcerting to some Americans, the less developed parts of the world would have more than 3/4 of the votes in such a parliament. This raises the question for many Americans of whether they really want democracy on the world level. Another problem for regional representation would be how to conduct voting on such a basis, especially since there are many languages and cultural differences in most regions. There would also be a problem of making sure that rules about who can vote and voting opportunities are the same throughout the region.

The Direct Election and Non-Governmental Organization Alternatives

These questions are especially relevant to the first proposed alternative, direct election of the members of the Second Assembly. There are also problems for the second proposed alternative where only persons especially registered for this particular election are allowed to vote. Such a system would greatly favor better educated persons. It doubles the difficulty of carrying out the election since in this case there must be not only equal opportunities to vote but also equal opportunities to register to vote. Also the election for the Second Assembly would need to be totally separate from any other elections since only a select group of people would be eligible to vote. In a separate world-wide election such as is being proposed the expense alone would become a factor. There would probably also be suspicions that these arrangements are being adopted just to make it difficult for the poorer countries to get a good representation.

The third proposed alternative was to have the members of the Second Assembly chosen by a special electoral college consisting of representatives of non-governmental organizations and institutions. But who would these people be? They would undoubtedly be predominantly from developed countries and the upper classes of the less developed countries. Who else has the time and money to be active in non-governmental organizations? Another critical issue will be which non-governmental organizations will be allowed to be involved in this process, and how will it be determined which organization gets how much weight in determining who will be in the electoral college? Representatives from certain non-governmental organizations might be informed and concerned about solving global problems, but there are other non-governmental organizations with different agendas. Questions can also be raised about how representative these non-governmental organizations are of the people of the world.

The fourth proposed alternative was that members of the Second Assembly could be selected by a commission of representatives of non-governmental organizations and institutions. But once again the question must be raised about which organizations and institutions and about who will decide which ones get to participate in the process. There has to be a suspicion that this kind of proposal is being made by a small group of people who suppose that they will be the ones doing the deciding. With this fourth proposal another kind of question comes into play. The whole idea of a Second Assembly was to have an institution which is more democratically selected than the present General Assembly. With this proposal there seems to be no very close connection between the people in general and the persons serving in the Second Assembly.

The European Model

The fifth version of the Second Assembly proposal uses the model of what happened in Europe with the European Parliament. The members of the European Parliament were originally members of the national parliaments selected by their colleagues. These parliamentarians had political power in their own countries and had an interest in strengthening the role of the European Parliament. This proved to be a good combination for getting the Parliament going and for seeing that it eventually would have some power, even after the switch was made to electing its members directly. It also gave the members of the national parliaments a desire to strengthen the European Community generally since they had a role in its development. The European Parliament still has nothing like the power of a national parliament, but its power is growing steadily, and it has become one of the main instruments supporting the federation of Europe. Another argument for this approach is that any creation of a Second Assembly will require the consent of the presently existing national governments. Giving some influence to persons who already have some political power in their own countries is much less likely to arouse opposition than proposals which would give political influence to people who lack political power within nations. (Supporters of the other proposals might respond that this is just the point of what they want to do, namely, get some influence into the hands of non-politicians!)

Dieter Heinrich, advocate of this fifth approach to a Second Assembly, indicates that there are some questions about it which need to be addressed. First, what is to be done in those countries which do not have democratic parliaments? One possibility is to give the responsibility to some other elected officials, possibly the mayors of the larger cities. He notes that they definitely

should not be appointed by the executive branch of government since that is how people get to be members of the General Assembly; such a procedure would undermine the whole rationale of the Second Assembly.

A second question to be addressed is whether the persons elected to serve in the Second Assembly by the national parliaments should themselves be members of those parliaments. That is how it was done in the European Parliament, but these parliamentarians are so busy with their national responsibilities that it is questionable how much time they would be able to give to their responsibilities in the Second Assembly. The national parliamentarians might have difficulty taking an oath to the global community. On the other hand, if the people to be chosen were not members of parliament, how enthusiastic would the parliamentarians be about the project? Such a departure from the European model might be fatal.

A third issue is whether the elections for members to the Second Assembly should be by secret ballot rather than open parliamentary debates where peer pressure and party politics might enter into the selection. But again, it may be dangerous to depart from the European model. It may be important that the people being selected for the Second Assembly have influence and not just respect within their own national parliaments.

Heinrich argues that parliamentarians, even though they are members of the political establishment within countries, will have a different outlook than the executive branch of government. This arrangement would also establish a desirable stronger link between national legislatures and the UN. He says: "A Parliamentary Assembly may be the single most important reform of the international system that could be undertaken at this time." The argument is that what worked in Europe should be tried at the global level.

*Drawing from Richards, I.A. **Nations and Peace**, Simon & Schuster, 1947.*

Election of People's Delegates

So far our discussion has focused on the idea of a Second Assembly at the UN. Now we need to look at another idea about how to make the UN more democratic, something which can be done within a nation. As we noted in the third sentence of this chapter, each nation is entitled to have five representatives in the UN General Assembly, but only one vote. It is unreasonable to expect that the administration in democratic countries would give up their practice of appointing their UN Ambassador or their prerogative of directing that Ambassador how to vote in the General Assembly. But it is possible that a less radical change might be accepted. Perhaps a system could be instituted where the whole country would be permitted to elect one of the five representatives to the UN General Assembly, what could be called "the

People's Delegate to the UN." It could be understood that this person would be a member of the nation's delegation to the UN but that s/he would not be able to decide alone how the nation would vote in the General Assembly.

What would be gained by electing a delegate with no voting power? First, there would be a national election for the post. People would need to decide for whom to vote. Different candidates would argue for different policies. Discussions of global issues would be the focus of debates among these candidates. The media could not ignore these issues. Voting would be based completely on these proposed global policies, uncontaminated by concerns about domestic issues. (A look at the history of American politics will show how people are elected on the basis of domestic considerations and we then get the foreign policy that President happens to support. And the same thing happens in other democracies.) The candidate who won could claim support from the voters for the policies s/he espoused.

If several countries were to elect "People's Delegates," then these delegates at the UN could form a caucus of "People's Delegates." They could get together and issue statements to the media. In one sense they would have no political power, but in another sense they would be able to claim legitimacy (they were elected) and they would be able to use the media to exert influence on policy. Other countries might decide to get into the act and elect their own "People's Delegate." Once there were enough of these "People's Delegates," their getting together would in a way begin to constitute a Second Assembly at the UN. In some more progressive countries the executive might even decide to appoint the

"People's Delegate" to be the official Ambassador to the UN.

This approach might be difficult to start in a country such as the U.S., but it seems quite feasible in some Scandinavian countries, some of the smaller democracies in Europe and elsewhere, and in progressive former British colonies such as Canada and New Zealand. If the idea got discussed in the U.S., it might get considerable support later after some other countries instituted it.

The ideas discussed here do not represent an exhaustive list of all the ways the UN might be made more democratic. You undoubtedly have some ideas of your own. Let others hear them. Your idea may be the very one we need to move toward a more democratic UN.

Discussion Questions

1. Do you favor a Second Assembly for a restructured United Nations?

2. Which kind of Second Assembly do you prefer -- directly elected? Representatives of non-governmental organizations?

3. Do you agree with the WFM proposal for a Parliamentary Assembly modeled after the European Parliamentary Assembly?

4. Do you favor direct election of "People's Delegates" to the UN General Assembly?

5. Is a more democratically elected world legislature an essential element of a New World Order under Law?

REFERENCES AND SUGGESTED READINGS

Best, Keith. "A Second Assembly for the UN?" **Canadian World Federalist.** (145 Spruce St., Ste. 207, Ottawa, Ontario K1R 6P1, Canada) May 1989, pp. 4-5.

Glossop, Ronald J. **Confronting War: An Examination of Humanity's Most Pressing Problem.** Jefferson, NC: McFarland, 1983, 1987, chps. XII & XVII.

Heinrich, Dieter. **Creating a World Parliament -- A Proposal for a United Nations General Assembly.** New York: World Assoc. for World Federation, 1990.

Morrow, Robert K. **Proposals for a More Equitable General Assembly Voting Structure.** Washington, DC: Center for UN Reform Education, 1989.

Newcombe, Hanna. **World Unification Plans and Analyses.** Dundas, Ontario, Canada: Peace Research Institute-Dundas, 1980.

Segall, Jeffrey. "Forum." **World Federalist News.** Washington, DC: World Federalist Association, Number 16 (April 1990), p. 7.

Segall, Jeffrey, et. al. **Proposal for a UN Second Assembly.** London, 1985.

Sohn, Louis B. **The United Nations: The Next Twenty-five years.** Dobbs Ferry, NY: Oceana, 1970.

Wynner, Edith and Georgia Lloyd (eds.). **Searchlight on Peace Plans: Choose Your Road to World Government.** New York: Dutton, 1944, 1949.

8. The Veto:
Abolition, Modification
or Preservation?

by Joseph Preston Baratta

UN Security Council condemning Iraq's annexation of Kuwait, Aug 90, UN photo 177065.

What Is the Veto?

BEFORE considering whether the U.N. Security Council veto should be abolished, modified, or left intact, which leads rapidly to questions of Charter amendment or interpretation and to the issue of comprehensive U.N. reform, we must be clear about what the veto is. Some speak of the veto as a "privilege" or even as a mark of the special status of nuclear powers, but in terms of the Charter the veto is a voting rule by which the Security Council exercises its primary *responsibility* for the maintenance of international peace and security (Art. 24). The Statement on Voting in the Security Council of 8 June 1945, by which the United States, United Kingdom, Soviet Union, China, and France sought to explain the veto, called it a "system of qualified majority voting."[1]

The voting rule is given in Art. 27 of the Charter:

  1. Each member of the Security Council shall have one vote.
  2. Decisions of the Security Council on procedural matters shall be made by an affirmative vote of nine members.
  3. Decisions of the Security Council on all other matters shall be made by an affirmative vote of nine members including the concurring votes of the permanent members; provided that, in decisions under Chapter VI, and under paragraph 3 of Article 52, a party to a dispute shall abstain from voting.

This language raises several points that those who would reform the veto should bear in mind: Representation in the Security Council is on the basis of one-state-one-vote, not one-person-one-vote, and the fifteen members represent all the states of the world.

"Decisions" generally refer to actions taken by the Security Council under Chap. VI (pacific settlement of disputes) and Chap. VII (action with respect to threats or breaches of the peace); decisions under Chap. VII are legally binding (Arts. 25, 48). Recommendations are not binding and hence are generally the province of the General Assembly (the most important decision, not requiring the concurrence of the Security Council, that the Assembly can take is approval of the budget).

Election of Judges to the International Court of Justice is shared between the General Assembly and the Security Council and is expressly exempt from the veto (Statute of the Court, Art. 10).

"Procedural" matters, to which the veto does not apply, generally include placing items on the agenda, inviting non-members of the Council to participate, and the like. Procedural matters are defined not by the Charter but by the Rules of Procedure (one idea for reform is to greatly modify the Rules). "All other matters" are understood as "substantive," on which the veto applies in full; the question whether a matter is procedural or substantive was understood in the San Francisco statement as itself substantive, and hence vetoable.

Nine of fifteen members is nearly a 2/3 majority. Originally the rule was seven of eleven, but the Security Council was enlarged to fifteen by Charter amendment in 1965 (a point to bear in mind when told the Charter cannot be amended).

The "permanent members" are the familiar Big Five, a relic of the Grand Alliance at the end of World War II. Changing world realities would today seem to most people to require that Germany and Japan, now major industrial powers under working democratic governments, be admitted to the exclusive club.

"Concurring votes" mean non-negative votes, including abstentions, after a precedent set in 1946 by the Soviet Union; absence from the Council chamber and "non-participation in the voting," favored by the Peoples Republic of China on old China issues, are treated as concurring.

Hence, only a negative vote by a permanent member is a veto. One veto, however, is sufficient to defeat an entire measure. Note that a veto may be cast against *any* resolution under Chap. VII, even one to which the permanent member is a party. Under Chap. VI (non-binding decisions or recommendations only), a permanent member who is a party to the dispute may not exercise its veto.

Why was the veto agreed to?

THIS voting rule affecting action under the authority of the United Nations was so important to the Allies in World War II and so difficult to formulate that its exact text was not agreed to by the Charter's drafters working in secret at Dumbarton Oaks in 1944, so it had to be settled by direct negotiation between Roosevelt, Stalin, and Churchill at Yalta in February 1945. At the San Francisco conference later in the spring of 1945, the five great powers to emerge from the war made it very clear to delegates from the smaller countries, to private advisors, and to consultants from citizens organizations like the American Association for the United Nations that without the veto there would be no U.N. organization at all.[2]

Nevertheless, there was much open opposition to the veto by delegates from the small powers, such as Herbert Evatt of Australia, Peter Frazer of New Zealand, and Carlos Romulo of the Philippines. Even China expressed its willingness "to delegate a part of our sovereignty to the new International Organization in the interests of collective security," which caused a hush in plenary session; within days the Big Three brought China around. France, newly restored to great power status, was equivocal.[3] World federalist observers such as Cord Meyer, Jr., and Grenville Clark wrote vigorous critiques of the veto as unfair and destructive of the whole system.[4]

But the veto was accepted as reflecting the "realities" of international relations at the time. If the five great powers could not agree on measures to maintain international peace and security, no paper pledge in the Charter could compel them to do so, and no international enforcement measures of the sort contemplated in Chap. VII could realistically be directed against a great power. That would be war waged by the U.N. community against a leading state. Hence the veto for such a case.

Readers interested in doing something about the veto should take a hard look at Chap. VII. The means of enforcement there are mainly military, of the sort to be applied to whole communities, not individuals. Art. 45, which provides for maintaining "national air-force contingents for combined international enforcement action," chillingly reveals what U.N. enforcement would really be. Bombing is to deter or stop aggressors. Apparently, air raids of the sort the Israelis launched against a suspected Iraqi nuclear reactor in 1981, or the U.S. nighttime air attack on a suspected terrorist headquarters in Tripoli in 1986, if they had been authorized by the Security Council are to become regular features of a U.N.-maintained "peace."

The recent Gulf War of 1990-91, which did have impressive U.N. backing under Chap. VII, more exactly exhibits the pattern. Iraq does not have a veto, and most people in allied coalition countries apparently felt that the war was justified to turn back Iraqi aggression. But how would Americans like it if, after some U.S. action of questionable international legality, like the mining of Nicaraguan harbors, the Security Council approved combined air operations against command and control centers in

Washington? The veto is a recognition of the futility of such international action. The problem, then, may lie not in Art. 27 but in Chap. VII. Until the world organization is vested with powers of legal enforcement action on individuals, perhaps by reform of Chap. XIV and the Statute of the International Court of Justice, the veto protects at least five nations and their many allies.

As qualified majority voting, the veto has significant implications for national sovereignty that are worth remembering. The Big Five alone, at the present stage of history, claim *absolute* national sovereignty in the sense that each may legally defy the remonstrances and actions of the entire international community. But this stance, fixed in Art. 27, is inconsistent with the first principle of the U.N., which is the "sovereign equality" of all members, as in Art. 2(1). All *other* states (the non-permanent members) have accepted majority rule, which implies limitations on their sovereignty or freedom of action, and even the Big Five have accepted majority rule, without any veto qualification, in *all* the other U.N. organs and agencies, such as the General Assembly and the International Monetary Fund. In the financial agencies like the IMF, votes are weighted in proportion to contributions, but majority rule is still observed. Hence, in principle outside the Security Council, all states accept limited sovereignty.

The veto, that is, a rule of unanimity among five powers within a 2/3 majority, is actually an advance on the voting rules of the old League of Nations, which required *complete unanimity* in its Council for substantive

decisions. Moreover, in the U.N. Security Council, decisions require the
concurrence of four non-permanent members, who temporarily in effect share
the veto power. With the enlargement
of the Security Council to fifteen, it
is possible, if all the permanent members abstain, do not participate, or
are absent, for a decision to be
reached *only* by non-permanent members,
which has happened in so important a
case as a December 1973 resolution
calling for peace in the Middle East.[5]
Even consensus decision making, increasing popular in the Security Council, can be regarded as further eroding the veto as a privilege of only
five states; some would say consensus
extends the veto to all.

What is the purpose of the veto?

THOSE who would strengthen the
U.N. must have a standard for their
proposals to meet, and this can only
be supplied by the purposes of the
organization. In the case of the
veto, its purpose is not expressly
stated, but the relevant purpose of
the organization as a whole is clearly
"to maintain international peace and
security" (Art. 1(1)). If the veto
contributes to this end, well and
good; if not, it should be changed.
There seems to be widespread agreement
among observers that the U.N. has
failed since 1945 to maintain international peace and security (32 international wars, 50 civil wars with foreign intervention,[6] only seven
exercises of collective security[7]),
but opinions differ on whether structural problems like the veto or the
current state of world politics is the
cause.

Evan Luard, an acute political
observer, finds that the veto has
brought "constant paralysis" to the
U.N. system, but he argues that "institutional changes" are not likely to
improve things without the willingness
of governments to use international
procedures. "It is not so much new
institutional arrangements as new attitudes that are needed," he

concludes.[8]

Sidney Bailey, another leading
U.N. scholar, quotes U.S. Ambassador
Charles Yost in 1967 with approval:
"I do not think the fault really lies
primarily in the Charter. I think it
lies in the policies of the various
governments."[9]

And Maurice Bertrand, former U.N.
inspector and currently the leading
advocate of U.N. reform, doubts, with
many other political scientists, that
the maintenance of international peace
and security was ever a realistic goal
that any international organization in
the contemporary world could attain by
"decisions" or "action." Bertrand
would leave the veto and indeed the
entire Security Council as is, for
Chap. VII is a deception, and he would
create new structures like an "Economic Security Council" as fora for the
negotiation of consensus on matters on
which the world can really agree, in
order to build up habits or *attitudes*
necessary for the actual settlement of
international conflict. New U.N.
structures rather on the model of the
European Community may be more effective for achieving the ultimate purposes of the United Nations than any
amount of tinkering with the veto

alone.[10]

"The primary purpose of the veto," Sidney Bailey states cynically after a lifetime observing the U.N., "is not to foster cooperation but to prevent action."[11] A more positive view might be stated as follows: The purpose of the veto is to prevent international enforcement action on aggressor states without the concurrence of the powers that must supply the bulk of the leadership, troops, supplies, and finances. The purpose is also to prevent enforcement against a great power itself, which would break up the U.N. That leaves a very narrow class of events (like the North Korean aggression in 1950 or the Iraqi case in 1990) which the world community can agree to suppress by military means.

The purpose of the veto, then, by preventing action disruptive of the tentative structures of an effective international organization, is to *permit* the development of consensus on both the pacific settlement of disputes (Chap. VI) and the enforcement of international authority (Chap. VII). The veto preserves some political space for the formation of international consensus on what is needed to maintain international peace and security.

The standard, then, for discussion of reform of the veto should be evident. It is a more effective United Nations as a whole. With that standard, the question before us becomes, not should the veto be abolished, for everyone who is not an isolationist agrees that it should, but *when?* In what degrees and with what other changes?

How has the veto actually worked historically?

TO FIND relief from theoretical quandaries, we might take a brief look at the history of use of the veto, which is not as dark as sometimes related. Despite early fears, the veto has not paralyzed the Security Council, though it has prevented the Council from taking effective decisions in such cases as the Vietnam War or the Soviet invasion of Afghanistan. From 1946 to 1987, according to Prof. Bailey's careful account, there were 242 vetoes.[12] But upwards of a thousand decisions have been taken, though many, indeed, were weaker and more ambiguous because of the threat or use of the veto.

A more meaningful measure is the number of items of which the Security Council has been seized to 1987. These come to 186 substantive matters. Of these 186, there were no vetoes on 127, and 70, or more than one third of the total, resulted in decisions. Another 32 items did suffer 180 vetoes, yet on those items some 459 resolutions or other decisions passed, as shown in Table 1.

Lastly, 27 items suffered 62 vetoes and never resulted in a positive decision. These include the issues of most political importance to the permanent members, such as Czechoslovakia in 1948 and 1968, the Berlin blockade in 1948, Grenada in 1983, and Nicaragua in 1982-86.

The Veto

Table 1
*Decisions and Vetoes by Security Council on Substantive
Proposals Regarding Peace and Security*

Subject	No. of Decisions	No. of Vetoes
Disarmament	8	3
Spanish question, 1946	3	4
Greece, 1946	7	6
Corfu Channel incidents, 1947	2	1
Indonesia, 1947	15	3
Middle East, 1948, 1967, 1976	239	24
India-Pakistan, 1948, 1971	23	5
Atomic energy	3	1
Korea, 1950	6	2
Guatemala, 1954	1	1
Suez Canal, 1956	1	1
Hungary, 1956	1	1
Lebanon, 1958	2	2
Congo, 1960	6	6
Southern Rhodesia, 1963	24	7
South Africa		
Namibia, 1968	27	7
Apartheit, 1977	27	6
Complaint by Angola, 1978	13	2
Latin America, 1973	2	1
Cyprus, 1974	42	1
Hostages in Iran, 1979	4	1
Afghanistan, 1980	1	1
Falklands/Malvinas, 1982	1	1
Nicaragua, 1985	1	1

Source: Bailey, *U.N. Security Council*, 211.

The tally of all vetoes is given in Table 2. The first U.S. veto was cast in March 1970 against a resolution concerning Southern Rhodesia. Thereafter, as the U.S. and its allies found themselves increasingly in a minority in the U.N., the United States has repeatedly had recourse to the veto, even while the Soviet Union's usage has fallen. This fact has softened Western historical criticism of Soviet "abuse" of the veto in early years. We are reminded why each of the Big Five insisted on the Yalta formula in 1945.

Table 2
Summary of Vetoes in the Security Council, 1946-1986

Member	1946-55	1956-65	1966-75	1976-86	Total
China	1	0	4	17	22
France	2	2	2	10	16
Soviet Union	77	26	11	7	121
U.K.	0	3	9	14	26
U.S.A.	0	0	12	45	57

Source: Bailey, *U.N. Security Council,* 209.

The veto has not prevented the Security Council from reaching agreement on over 74 resolutions without a vote, that is, by consensus, since 1946. Since construction of private chambers behind the public meeting room at U.N. headquarters (a gift of the Federal Republic of Germany after admission in 1973), the Council has had much more recourse to private meetings and processes of conciliation for the resolution of conflicts.[13]

Lastly, the Uniting for Peace Resolution of November 1950, which provided continuing U.N. authority for the "police action" in Korea after the Soviet delegate returned to his seat, provides an important precedent for avoiding the veto. The resolution provides that, when the Security Council cannot act to stop aggression "because of lack of unanimity of the permanent members" (that is, because of the veto), the General Assembly may make "appropriate recommendations to Members for collective measures...." After Korea, the Uniting for Peace Resolution has been invoked on six occasions: to establish the U.N. Emergency Force of 1956 (the first peacekeeping force), to call for a withdrawal of Soviet forces from Hungary in 1956 (ignored), to settle a question between Lebanon and Jordan, to deal with the situation in the Congo after 1960, to deal with the India-Pakistan war of 1971, and to condemn the Soviet invasion of Afghanistan in 1980.[14]

What are the alternatives for choice in reform of the veto?

IN GENERAL, there are three alternatives: (1) outright abolition, usually proposed in conjunction with systemic Charter amendment; (2) modification, either by amendment of Art. 27 or by changes elsewhere in the Charter that have the effect of increasing the scope of unqualified majority rule, as by adding new permanent members to the Security Council or by changing the voting rules in the General Assembly to increase its competence; or (3) leaving the veto intact but pursuing political changes that cause the Big Five to voluntarily restrict their use of the veto, which would remain as an ultimate safeguard.

The historical tendency of reform proposals is now heavily weighted toward the third alternative, since, like Edmund Burke, most international statespersons and commentators have grown very suspicious of world revolutionary projects. But Charter amendment has already been accomplished in enlarging the Security Council (1965) and the Economic and Social Council (1965, 1973), the review conference promised in Art. 109 is still pending, and someday "we the peoples" must face up to bringing our fundamental law into conformity with our principles and purposes. In the wake of the Gulf War, talk of a "new world order" invites serious public reflection on its meaning.

What are some specific proposals of veto reform?

Abolition. Grenville Clark and Louis B. Sohn in *World Peace through World Law* (1958) dispense with the veto. In place of the Security Council, they would create an Executive Council of seventeen responsible to a popularly representative General Assembly; decisions of the new Council on "important" matters would require a vote of any fourteen (almost 3/4), while "others" would require eleven (almost 2/3). The basis of their plan is a clear philosophy of popular sovereignty, which requires changes to the entire Charter in order to transform it into a constitution for a limited world federation.[15] In my opinion, only reforms of this magnitude are adequate to the world's problems of the 21st century, but to consider the whole Clark-Sohn plan would take us too far afield from the veto.

The McCloy-Zorin Agreement on the Principles for Disarmament Negotiations of 1961, which established the objective of "general and complete disarmament under effective international control," expressly provided that the requisite international disarmament organization should *not* be subject to the U.N. Security Council veto during verification.[16] The American and Soviet draft treaties on disarmament that followed in 1962, though established "within the framework of the United Nations" (where the veto would still apply), provided for majority voting in the disarmament organization by carefully designed stages.[17] An up-to-date draft disarmament treaty by Marcus Raskin (1986) does not tamper with the veto, but once the world were totally disarmed the veto would have very little meaning.[18]

China on occasion expresses willingness to abolish the veto, arguing that this would lead to greater democratization in the Council.[19]

The United States once, in the Baruch plan, proposed to abolish the veto in matters relating to the international control of atomic energy (1946).[20]

Modification. The Special Committee on the Charter of the United Nations and on the Strengthening of the Role of the Organization, established by the General Assembly in 1975, has conducted the most thoroughgoing review of official state proposals to amend the Charter or to improve its effectiveness under the existing text. There have been proposals both to abolish the veto and to modify it. The Philippines proposed abolition in "matters not involving enforcement action, including peace-keeping by interposition." Colombia suggested abolition in "the case of appointments of commissions of inquiry or fact-finding missions or commissions to serve humanitarian purposes." Romania suggested that the rule that permanent members who are parties to a conflict shall abstain from Chap. VI decisions be extended to Chap. VII, and that each geographic region send in rotation one or two representatives, with veto, to the Security Council. Mexico proposed adding at least one permanent member from a Third World country on a rotating basis, with the same prerogatives as the others. The U.N. Secretary General reviewed ninety similar proposals in 1976, but no *constitutional* change affecting the responsibility of the great powers has ever been accepted. The political issues, however, have been raised.[21]

Japan has been in the lead in subsequent years to increase the size of the Security Council by five permanent members without veto. Candidates commonly mentioned are Japan, Germany, India, Nigeria, and Brazil. Arguments pro are that this would provide greater continuity for a representative from each of the major geographical regions, would end the anachronism of the privileged World War II victors, would not produce a body too large to conduct business, would not increase potential for paralysis due to the veto, and would not require a current permanent member to concur in a plan to reduce its own status. Arguments

con are that this would create three classes of membership and would further dilute the influence of the present permanent members, since even now measures can carry with the votes of members lacking a veto. But this, I think, might be just the tactic to break down in an evolutionary way the mystique attached to unanimity among the Big Five.[22]

Austria, in comprehensive proposals to enhance the effectiveness of the Security Council made in 1972, proposed re Art. 27 that the number of matters now classed as "procedural," where the veto does not apply, be enlarged. Which matters should be so designated Austria did not say but suggested that the Council determine them politically by consensus. In principle, all of Chap. VI, and even Chap. VII, could be treated as "procedural." This might in practice eliminate a highly artificial distinction, which exists nowhere else in the U.N. system.[23]

The Rules of Procedure, last amended in 1982, could also be changed to similar effect, without touching the Charter, as Prof. Bailey ingeniously shows.[24]

The Commission to Study the Organization of Peace, basing their ideas on the fundamental objective of developing world law and international law, proposed a three-stage process moving deliberately toward abolition. Prof. Sohn and others suggested that, first, the permanent members should relinquish their right of veto only with respect to peaceful settlement under Chap. VI; the voting rule, then, should be changed to require a concurring vote of both a majority of the permanent members and a majority of the nonpermanent. Second, the veto should be removed with respect to enforcement under Chap. VII, as for peacekeeping, when the measures do not involve armed force under U.N. authority. Thirdly, the veto should be relinquished completely under Chap. VII, and the voting rule changed as above for Chap. VI, provided that no state should be required to use armed force without its consent.[25]

Richard Hudson's Binding Triad proposal would not eliminate the Security Council veto, but it would so strengthen the General Assembly that the effect would nearly be the same. Hudson, in order to escape the dilemmas of an Assembly based on sovereign equality but unreflective of the realities of power and a Council where great power unanimity can rarely be achieved, proposes that the General Assembly be vested with the power to reach binding decisions if concurrent 2/3 majorities of states, populations, and wealth can be reached. Amendments to Arts. 13 and 18 would be all that is required. The Security Council would remain responsible for enforcement, but the "higher quality" of Assembly resolutions reached by the new formula, practice sessions have shown, would obviate the need in most cases for military measures.[26]

Political changes. Lastly, there is a class of proposals that, while not formally changing the Charter, would improve the use of the "existing machinery," including the veto. There have been, for instance, calls for voluntary restraint, for strengthening other organs like the General Assembly or the Secretariat by ingenious interpretation of the Charter, for creating whole new "subsidiary organs" under Arts. 22 and 29, and especially for

new national policies that recognize the *common interest* in international institutions to resolve disputes peacefully.

As fear and resistance to reform of the U.N. began to dissipate in the 1980s, there was increased interest in so modest a device as increasing the Secretary General's role in fact-finding, global watch, and other anticipatory functions, while leaving the Security Council, with the veto intact, to take action or to desist as before. In his 1982 *Report on the Work of the Organization,* Secretary General Javier Pérez de Cuéllar proposed:

In order to carry out effectively the preventive role foreseen for the Secretary General under Article 99, I intend to develop a wider and more systematic capacity for fact-finding in potential conflict areas. . . . Moreover, the Council itself could devise more swift and responsive procedures for sending good offices missions, military or civilian observers or a United Nations presence to areas of potential conflict.[27]

Increased fact-finding capacity, by the Secretary General or by the Security Council, has been discussed at length in the Special Committee on the Charter. Fact-finding, in Chap. VI terms, belongs with inquiry as a pacific means of settlement. Another proposal would increase the role of mediation. The Special Committee by the end of the 1980s was still considering a proposal to establish under the General Assembly and the Secretary General, where the veto would be relaxed, a "commission of good offices, mediation, and conciliation." The idea of the Security Council going

into action before, not after, a conflict erupts is also behind the "global watch" proposals of the UNA-USA
(below).[28]

Secretary Pérez de Cuéllar limits
his proposals on the veto to the political dimension:

> Adequate working relations between
> the permanent members of the Secur-
> ity Council are a *sine qua non* of
> the Council's effectiveness. What-
> ever their relations may be outside
> the United Nations, within the
> Council the permanent members,
> which have special rights and spe-
> cial responsibilities under the
> Charter, share a sacred trust that
> should not go by default owing to
> their bilateral difficulties. When
> this happens, the Council and
> therefore the United Nations are
> the losers, since the system of
> collective security envisaged by
> the Charter presupposes at the min-
> imum, a working relationship among
> the permanent members. I appeal to
> the members of the Council, espe-
> cially its permanent members, to
> reassess their obligations in that
> regard and to fulfil them at the
> high level of responsibility indi-
> cated in the Charter.[29]

That the Cold War has ended since
these words were written does not
change the fundamental political truth
expressed in them.

The Soviet Union has not softened
its stance against eliminating the
veto, but Pres. Gorbachev, in his historic 1987 *Pravda* article, did propose
holding more meetings of the Security
Council at the foreign minister's level, occasional meetings in regions of
friction and tension and in the

capitals of the permanent members, and
special missions to areas of conflict
to implement Council decisions. He
also approved the Final Document of
the First Special Session of the U.N.
General Assembly on Disarmament
(1978), which incorporates the principles of the McCloy-Zorin agreement.[30]

The United States under the Bush
administration shows no sign of relax-
ing the veto, but Pres. Carter in 1978
approved "fact-finding missions as a
procedural matter not subject to veto,
so long as mandates are clear and non-
prejudicial." Secretary of State
Vance added that the U.S. was also
prepared to join with other permanent
members to change the 1945 statement
applying the veto to questions of de-
fining the area of procedural matters,
and he supported Japan's proposal for
increased permanent seats, though he
was silent on whether that would include veto powers.[31]

Brian Urquhart, in the aftermath
of the Gulf War, has made impressive
political proposals for a truly effective collective security system. He
urges increased coordination and con-
sultation among governments within the
U.N., developing a global watch function, more anticipatory action by the
Security Council, and improved implementation of Council decisions in the
fields of peacemaking (Chap. VI),
peacekeeping (Chap. "VI and 1/2"),
enforcement (Chap. VII), and response
to unconventional situations like terrorism and hostage taking.[32]

The Palme Commission in its influ-
ential report, *Common Security* (1982),
proposed a "concordat" or understanding among the permanent members not to
exercise their veto in collective security operations designed to prevent

settlement by force of border disputes or threats to territorial integrity in Third World countries, like Iraq and Kuwait. The intent here was to open up all of the U.N.'s anticipatory, preventive, and enforcement capabilities. A staged process was envisaged, proceding from a fact-finding mission to a military observer team to U.N. military forces. Because such measures would be limited to the Third World, it was thought the great powers could relinquish their veto without danger to themselves. When the South was policed, then the North could accept similar measures.[33]

Maurice Bertrand has conducted the most informed recent critique of the U.N. system. He finds that international decision making, at the present stage of world consensus on values, is effective only in the field of humanitarian and technical activities (High Commissioner for Refugees, Universal Postal Union, etc.); in the fields of peace and security, economic development, and the global "problematique," what is needed is new negotiation structures in order to *reach* consensus. Hence, he argues, "it is pointless to try to modify the structure of the Security Council." Bertrand would temporarily abandon hope for progress in the U.N.'s maintenance of international peace and security, so he proposes to transform the Economic and Social Council into an "Economic Security Council" and to strengthen fora on the problematique like the 1992 U.N. Conference on Environment and Development. Full consideration of his shrewd proposals would take us back into comprehensive U.N. reform, for which this chapter is not the place.[34]

The United Nations Association's elaborate proposal, *A Successor Vision* (1988), was guided by the work of Bertrand, who was a senior consultant. Its recommendations -- to establish a Ministerial Board of 25 governments, expansion of the Economic and Social Council to plenary size, elimination of the General Assembly's Second and Third Committees, merger of the Special Political and Fourth Committees, and the like -- passed political tests for acceptability and were all within the competence of the General Assembly, the Economic and Social Council, and the Secretariat, without necessity for Charter amendment. On the veto, the UNA panel who authored the work took the view that "the path to more effective management of security issues lies not through 'better' voting but, rather, through less emphasis on voting itself as a means of solving intractable problems." Their larger solutions, again, would take us beyond the scope of this chapter.[35]

The newest and most impressive political proposal touching the veto is the April 1991 Stockholm Initiative on Global Security and Governance, *Common Responsibility in the 1990s,* which continues the tradition of *Common Crisis, Common Security,* and *Our Common Future.* The new initiative, signed by Willy Brandt, Gro Harlem Brundtland, Ingvar Carlsson, Shridath Ramphal, Jimmy Carter, Robert McNamara, Eduard Shevardnadze, Julius Nyerere, and other leaders from around the world, deals with large issues of peace and security, development, environment, population, human rights, and "global governance." On the Security Council, the leaders propose "that its composition and the use of the veto be reviewed."

Recommendations

REFORM of the veto is clearly not simply a matter of changing Art. 27 in which a few unfortunate words appear ("concurrence. . ."), but of transforming the entire Charter and with it the nature of international relations. In accordance with most recent observers, I would recommend changes in national policies toward the U.N. for now. Nations must, as Evan Luard says, develop new "attitudes," and governments, as Amb. Yost said, must recognize the "fault" in their own policies. Prof. Bailey aptly expresses the reasoning that must be conveyed to national elites in order to make their policies more cooperative: "All States and all regions stand to gain from a firmer and more humane international order in which the short-term national advantage is not pursued to the limit if to do so frustrates the universal common good."[36]

Hence, U.S. recourse to the U.N. in the interests of a "new world order," as in the recent Gulf War, ought not to stop short of U.N. command for joint forces under Arts. 42 and 47, where the veto continues to apply. Very possibly, as in Pres. Carter's proposals, the veto could be relaxed enough to elevate fact-finding to a procedural issue. If that had been done long ago, the Secretary General would have had the power to deploy observer missions on the borders of Kuwait and Iraq, avoiding the eventual conflict. Soviet suggestions to convene the Security Council more often at the ministerial level or to meet in foreign capitals would enhance its authority; proposals to dispatch more observer missions would improve its early warning capability. The Secretary General is right to emphasize not the privilege, but the responsibility, of the permanent members.

As the world atmosphere clears, it should be possible for the permanent members to exercise voluntary restraint in their use of the veto on questions of the admission of new members to the U.N., appointment of the Secretary General, and peaceful settlement of disputes (Chap. VI). New permanent members (Japan, Germany, India, Nigeria, Brazil) would bring the Council closer to reality fifty years after World War II, but these new permanent members ought not to receive vetoes, which are destructive of majority rule. The Palme concordat against the Third World should be rejected as inequitable and oppressive. The process suggested by the Commission to Study the Organization of Peace for staged elimination of the veto is reasonable, but the same effect may be achieved within a much larger, more complex process of evolution.

Structural reform, of the sort contemplated in coherent proposals by Maurice Bertrand, the UNA panel that produced *A Successor Vision,* or Grenville Clark and Louis B. Sohn, should be saved for another historic moment when, in Tom Paine's words, we have it in our power to make the world over again. One such opportunity might come in 1999, which has been recommended as the date for a third general peace conference, reminiscent of the Hague peace conferences or the conferences on international organization following the world wars, as the fitting conclusion of the U.N. Decade of International Law and the inauguration of the third millenium.

Endnotes

Joseph P. Baratta is a historian of international organization. He has worked as U.N. Representative of the World Federalist Movement (WAWF) and has written on international verification, peacekeeping, arbitration, and human rights in monographs available from the Center for U.N. Reform Education.

1.   Quoted in Sidney D. Bailey, *The Procedure of the U.N. Security Council* (Oxford: Clarendon, 2nd ed. 1988), 402.

2.   Carlos Romulo, *Romulo: A Third World Soldier at the U.N.* (New York: Praeger, 1986), 13-17.

3.   *The United Nations Conference on International Organization, San Francisco, California, April 25 - June 26, 1945, Selected Documents* (Washington: Department of State, Conference Series 83, Pub. 2490, 1946), 147-51, 257, 740-42.

4.   Cord Meyer, Jr., "A Serviceman Looks at the Peace," *Atlantic,* September 1945, 43-48; Grenville Clark, "The Dumbarton Oaks Proposals -- An Analysis," *American Bar Association Journal,* 30 (December 1944): 667-73.

5.   Davidson Nicol et al., *The United Nations Security Council: Toward Greater Effectiveness* (New York: UNITAR, E.82.XV.CR/15, 1982), 106.

6.   Also 15 border conflicts and 53 civil wars. Hanna Newcomb, *Design for a Better World* (Lanham, MD: University Press of America, 1983), 231-34.

7.   Cease-fire in Palestine (July 1948); Korean War (1950-53); mandatory sanctions against Rhodesia (May 1968); extension of these sanctions (March 1970); decision against South African rights in Namibia (January 1970); sanctions on arms trade to South Africa (1977); Gulf War (1990-91). Evan Luard, *The United Nations: How It Works and What It Does* (New York: St. Martin's, 1979), 23; David J. Scheffer, *The United Nations in the Culf Crisis and Options for U.S. Policy* (New York: UNA-USA, Occasional Paper No. 1, February 1991), 7-11.

8.   Luard, *United Nations,* 11, 28.

9.   Bailey, *U.N. Security Council,* 7.

10.   Maurice Bertrand, *The Third Generation World Organization* (Dordrecht and Boston: Martinus Nijhoff, 1989), 83-90.

11.   Bailey, *U.N. Security Council,* 160.

12.   Bailey, *U.N. Security Council,* 200-214.

13.   Bailey, *U.N. Security Council,* 355.

14.   Michael Howard, "The United Nations and International Security," in Adam Roberts and Benedict Kingsbury, eds., *United Nations: Divided World* (Oxford: Clarendon, 1988), 34; Bailey, *U.N. Security Council,* 245, 444; A/RES/ES-6/2, 14 January 1980.

15.   Grenville Clark and Louis B. Sohn, *World Peace through World Law* (Cambridge: Harvard University Press, 1958, 1960, 1966), Art. 27 and comment.

16.   Jozef Goldblat, *Arms Control: A Survey and Appraisal of Multilateral Agreements* (London: Taylor & Francis, Stockholm International Peace Research Institute, 1978), 75-76.

17.   Treaties reprinted in Seymour Melman, ed., *Disarmament: Its Politics and Economics* (Boston: American Academy of Arts and Sciences, 1962), 282, 291-92, 328-30.

18.   Marcus Raskin, Draft Treaty for a Comprehensive Program for Common Security and General Disarmament (Washington: Institute for Policy Studies,

1986).

19.   Nicol, *U.N. Security Council,* 105.

20.   Joseph Preston Baratta, "Was the Baruch Plan a Proposal of World Government?" *International History Review,* 7 (1985): 592-621.

21.   Analytical Study submitted by the Secretary General pursuant to General Assembly resolution 3499 (XXX), 2 February 1976, A/AC.182/-L.2, paragraphs 64-73; *Report of the Special Committee on the Charter of the United Nations and on the Strengthening of the Role of the Organization,* General Assembly Official Records, 32nd session, Supplement No. 33, 1977, A/32/33, pp. 131-38, 198-99.

22.   Nicol, *U.N. Security Council,* 13-15.   Cf.   Arthur Lall, *The Security Council in a Universal United Nations* (New York: Carnegie Endowment for International Peace, 1971); Bailey, *U.N. Security Council,* 157-61.

23.   Quoted in Nicol, *U.N. Security Council,* Appendix III.

24.   Bailey, *U.N. Security Council,* 334-53.

25.   Louis B. Sohn and the Commission to Study the Organization of Peace, *The United Nations: The Next Twenty-Five Years* (Dobbs Ferry, NY: Oceana, 1970), 60-61.

26.   Richard Hudson, *The Case for the Binding Triad,* Special Study No. 7 (1983), Center for War/Peace Studies, 218 East 18th Street, New York, NY 10002.

27.   Javier Pérez de Cuéllar, *Report of the Secretary General on the Work of the Organization,* 7 September 1982, A/37/1.

28.   *Report of the Special Committee on the Charter,* GAOR, Sup. 33, 1979, A/34/33, p/ 5; 1980, A/35/33, p. 22; 1985, A/40/33, pp. 6-16.

29.   Pérez de Cuéllar, *Report.*

30.   Mikhail Gorbachev, "The Reality and Guarantee of a Secure World," *Pravda* and *Izvestia,* 17 September 1987.

31.   United States, Department of State, *Reform and Restructuring of the U.N. System* (Washington: Dept. of State, International Organization and Conference Series 135, Pub. 8940, June 1978), 7, 15.

32.   Brian Urquhart, "Learning from the Gulf," *New York Review of Books,* 7 March 1991, 34-37.

33.   Olaf Palme and the Independent Commission on Disarmament and Security Issues, *Common Security: Blueprint for Survival* (New York: Simon & Schuster, 1982), 162-64.

34.   Bertrand, *Third Generation World Organization,* 83; see especially Annex I, which reprints his 1985 Report, A/40/988.

35. U.N. Management and Decision-Making Project Panel, Peter J. Fromuth, ed., *A Successor Vision: The United Nations of Tomorrow* (Lanham, MD: University Press of America, UNA-USA, 1988), 63.

36.   Bailey, *U.N. Security Council,* 354.

Bibliography

Bailey, Sidney D. *The Procedure of the U.N. Security Council*. Oxford: Clarendon, 2nd ed., 1988.

Bertrand, Maurice. *The Third Generation World Organization*. Dordrecht and Boston: Martinus Nijhoff, 1989.

Clark, Grenville, and Sohn, Louis B. *World Peace throught World Law*. Cambridge, MA: Harvard University Press, 1958, 1960, 1966.

Luard, Evan. *The United Nations: How It Works and What It Does*. New York: St. Martin's, 1979.

Nicol, Davidson, et al. *The United Nations Security Council: Toward Greater Effectiveness*. New York: UNITAR, 1982.

Palme, Olaf, and the Independent Commission on Disarmament and Security Issues. *Common Security: Blueprint for Survival*. New York: Simon & Schuster, 1982.

Pérez de Cuéllar, Javier. *Report of the Secretary General on the Work of the Organization*. 7 September 1982. A/37/1.

Roberts, Adam, and Kingsbury, Benedict, eds. *United Nations: Divided World*. Oxford: Clarendon, 1988.

Special Committee on the Charter of the United Nations and on the Strengthening of the Role of the Organization. *Report*. General Assembly Official Records, 32nd Session, Supplement No. 33, 1977. A/32/33.

Sohn, Louis B., and the Commission to Study the Organization of Peace. *The United Nations: The Next Twenty-Five Years*. Dobbs Ferry, NY: Oceana, 1970.

Stockholm Initiative on Global Security and Governance. *Common Responsibility in the 1990s*. 22 April 1991. Distributed by the World Federalist Assn.

U.N. Management and Decision-Making Project Panel, Peter J. Fromuth, ed. *A Successor Vision: The United Nations of Tomorrow*. Lanham, MD: University Press of America, UNA-USA, 1988.

Urquhart, Brian. "Learning from the Gulf." *New York Review of Books*. 7 March 1991.

Discussion Questions

1. Which of the alternatives for the reform of the veto do you prefer?

2. How should the veto be modified, in your opinion, given the present U.N. structure?

3. At what point do you think the veto should be abolished?

4. What other changes in the Charter or in national policy should be made if the veto is abolished?

5. What role, if any, should the Security Council play in a restructured U.N. or world federation?

9. The Secretary-General: Should His Role Be Enhanced?

by Jack Yost

The role of the Secretary-General of the United Nations is unique to represent the interests of all humanity. As such, the leadership of the Secretary-General is crucial for solving the increasingly complex and interconnected problems of our times. In <u>A World in Need of Leadership</u>, two distinguished former UN officials, Brian Urquhart and Erskine Childers write: "The pressing need and the present opportunity for well-directed international cooperation demand the best possible leadership for the United Nations system, the only existing universal framework for intergovernmental cooperation and international management. This is a testing time for the organization of the UN system. It is a time when wise transnational leadership is vital for human well-being--perhaps even for human survival."

In order to provide such leadership, however, the position of the Secretary-General must be strengthened in important ways. The UN Charter assigns two principal functions to the Secretary-General: one political and the other administrative. Significant reform is needed in both these broad areas of responsibility.

The political role of the Secretary-General, which includes peace-making and peace-keeping, has never been very clearly defined. In practice, it has depended very much on the character and initiative of the individual. Under Article 33 of the Charter, which requires the parties to a dispute to seek a solution by peaceful means, the Secretary-General has traditionally acted as a neutral broker through the use of what is known as his "good offices." In cooperation with the Security Council, he can send special representatives on fact-finding missions or to help mediate conflicts or he can intervene personally. His success depends a great deal on whether or not he commands the full respect of the parties to a dispute. He must not only be impartial but must be perceived to be so.

Two Reforms Needed

Reforms in the way the Secretary-General is selected could greatly enhance universal respect for the office. Under the Charter, the Security Council recommends the candidate for Secretary-General for appointment by the General Assembly. In practice, the process is both unseemly and inadequate, involving back-room politics, campaigning for the office by individuals, and no organized search for the most

Perez de Cuellar, UN Secretary-General, 1981-91.

outstanding candidate. Since the five permanent members enjoy veto power over the selection, finding a candidate on whom they all agree tends to eliminate risk-takers and strong personalities and to favor mediocre, compromise candidates. Reforms should include:

1) a single seven-year term of office. Seven years is long enough for making a significant contribution to the organization, but not too long for such a physically and mentally strenuous job. The one term limitation frees the Secretary-General from the need to curry favor with certain governments for re-election.

2) a proper search process. To find the best possible candidate, the Security Council should appoint a special search committee made up of eminent persons, which would be authorized to seek information and advice from any source, including private organizations and the international civil service.

In their Report, Urquhart and Childers recommend the establishment of such a group:

"The search group would examine the qualifications and background of all nominees, with the option to interview them and, if necessary, to conduct a wider search for candidates. It should consult with the regional groups, and its recommendations should reflect, among other things, their views.

"The right to nominate candidates should be clearly defined, as well as the information required to accompany a nomination. A timetable for the whole process, including deadlines for the nomination of candidates, should also be agreed on.

"The aim of such arrangements would be to produce a better considered choice of candidates, to avoid a desperate last-minute search for a compromise candidate, and to give more weight to the views of the membership as a whole, as well as of concerned constituencies outside the UN."

Fact-Finding and Early Warning Technology

Article 99 of the Charter authorizes the Secretary-General to bring to the attention of the Security Council any matter which in his opinion may threaten the maintenance of international peace and security. Here the Charter clearly envisages someone with the power to anticipate and prevent crises. To do this, the Secretary-General's preventive role needs to be significantly strengthened, and essential to such prevention is fact-finding, the ability to track potential trouble spots around the world.

In 1991, the Charter Committee (the Special Committee on the Charter of the UN and the Strengthening of the Role of the Organization) finished its work of several years on UN fact-finding and issued a Draft Declaration on Fact-Finding. Although non-binding in nature, the declaration recognizes that the ability of the UN to maintain international peace and security depends on timely, comprehensive and objective information about disputes and conflicts. It urges that when facts cannot be obtained through existing means, "fact-finding missions should be undertaken" by the Secretary-General, the Security Council, or the General Assembly. "The Secretary-General should monitor the state of international peace and security in order to provide early warning of disputes," the report says. "He should make full use of the information gathering capabilities of the

Secretariat and bring all relevant information to the attention of the Security Council or General Assembly."

While such a declaration is important, it does not spell out exactly how its recommendations can be implemented. While the UN Office of Research and Collection of information exists to provide the Secretary-General with timely news, it has very limited funds, resources and personnel.

Commenting on his need for adequate early warning, Perez de Cuellar pointed out in a July, 1991 interview that he has no satellites at his disposal. Had he one, he would have been informed about the 100,000 Iraqi soldiers on the Iraq-Kuwait border, which would have enabled him to warn members of the Security Council. He expressed the hope that his "successor will have more success with this" and have "more authority for the office of the Secretary-General."

In a speech he gave at Oxford in 1986, Perez de Cuellar elaborated on this theme: "In today's world, neither the functions of the Secretary-General nor multilateral diplomacy should be limited to good offices or negotiation. One of the UN's duties in a crisis is to be alert to all the nuances, and to use its contacts with governments to try to allay the underlying fears and suspicions. This requires a conscious decision on the part of the member states to strengthen the role of the Secretary-General and to provide him with better means to keep a watch over actual and potential points of conflict. At present, the UN lacks independent sources of information: its means of obtaining up-to-date information are primitive by comparison with those of member states-- and indeed of most transnational corporations. To judge whether a matter

may threaten international peace and security, the Secretary-General needs more than news reports and analyses made by outside experts; he needs full and impartial data, and he needs to be able to monitor developments world wide."

Regional Representatives Suggested

Besides improved technical resources, such as satellites, the Secretary-General should have regional representatives or ambassadors, whose specific mission is to keep him informed of political developments.

In the aftermath of the Gulf War, momentum for reform in this area has been building. The Stockholm Initiative on Global Security and Governance, signed by 36 renowned world leaders, says, "The Secretary-General should have the power to take initiatives and act swiftly when an international crisis calls for it, if need be without prior consent by the Security Council. For this to be possible he needs access also to the means, as well as the authority to begin creating a real preventive machinery."

Three More Proposed Changes

Three other changes could enhance the political effectiveness of the Secretary-General in preventing conflict.

First, the Secretary-General should be granted authority--which at present belongs to both the General Assembly and the Security Council--to request from the International Court of Justice advisory opinions of the legal aspects of a dispute. An advisory opinion in such a case would help clarify the nature of the conflict and provide the Secretary-General added authority for the use of his good offices.

Second, the Secretary-General should meet with the Security Council on a regular basis--preferably once a week--to review the international situation in order to defuse and prevent crises.

Third, the Secretary-General should be given authority to establish a voluntary fund--to which the public and private organizations could contribute--for use at his discretion in carrying out his peace-making and peace-keeping duties. While such a fund would not solve the problem of providing sufficient financing for growing UN peace-keeping activities, it would allow the Secretary-General to act with more speed and flexibility.

While the Charter speaks very generally of the political and administrative roles of the Secretary-General, the position has evolved to include a broad range of specific tasks. They include, as outlined by Urquhart and Childers:

--administration and management of the Secretariat;

--official representation of the United Nations worldwide;

--constant contact with member states;

--representation and interpretation of the United Nations to the public, and to the non-governmental sector and the private sector;

--coordination of the UN system;

--maintenance of a global watch on major developments;

--generating ideas and strategies;

--use of good offices and crisis management (peace-making and peace-keeping);

--good offices on human rights and humanitarian matters.

Such responsibilities are clearly beyond the scope of any single individual, Urquhart and Childers continue, and require future Secretaries-General to work through the managed delegation of authority in the United Nations itself to a far greater extent and in a far more effective way than in the past. Such delegation of authority is impossible without important reform of the UN Secretariat itself.

Reorganization of the Secretariat

At present, the Secretariat is, quite literally, an organizational nightmare, with some 30 units reporting directly to the Secretary-General. In such a situation, careful monitoring of the work of so many units in order to provide direction, facilitate cooperation and prevent overlapping and duplication of work is clearly impossible.

In a 1991 monograph, Reorganization of the Secretariat, Erskine Childers recommends that the disparate offices and departments be consolidated into four major departments, namely: 1) Political, Security and Peace Affairs, 2) Economic, Social, Development and Environment Affairs, 3) Humanitarian Affairs and Human Rights, and 4) Administration, Management, and Conference Services. This reform would reduce the number of senior officials advising, and reporting directly to, the Secretary-General, as well as help streamline operations.

Moreover, the current top structure of authority under the Secretary-General is sadly inadequate to meet the demands of the office. Childers recommends the creation of an Executive Office, headed by an official senior enough to apply the authority of the Secretary-General, for the functions assigned to it. Such an office would serve as the central reporting and information point for the Secretary-General, coordinate the Secretariat's substantive paperwork, supervise public relations matters concerning the Secretary-General, review communications addressed to the office, and serve as liaison to the other departments.

During the last few years, as the United Nations has taken on more responsibilities, a consensus has developed among most governments on the need to reform and streamline the operations of the Secretariat. Such reform is crucial for far more than effective administration. It will help liberate the Secretary-General for his most important roles: to serve as a moral compass for the world community, to mediate and prevent conflicts, and to provide dynamic leadership for the United Nations organization as a whole.

Discussion Questions

1. Do you favor a single seven-year term for the Secretary-General, or do you prefer the present five-year renewable term?

2. Should a Secretary-General have access to satellites as part of an early warning system?

3. Should the Secretary-General be given the authority (by the General Assembly) to seek advisory opinions from the International Court of Justice?

4. Should the Secretary-General be the chief executive if the UN is transformed into a world federation, or should that role be fulfilled by the Security Council?

REFERENCES AND SUGGESTED READINGS

Childers, Erskine. "Reorganization of the UN Secretariat, A Suggested Outline." Unpublished monograph, 1991.

de Cuellar, Perez. "The Role of the United Nations Secretary-General." Cyril Foster Lecture, Oxford University, 1986. (Copy available through UN Office of Public Information)

Urquhart, Brian, and Childers, Erskine, **A World in Need of Leadership.** Ford Foundation, 1991. (Free copies available from Ford Foundation, 320 E. 43rd St., New York, NY 10017)

10. UN Funding:
Supplemental or Direct Taxation?

by Mark Yakich

The UN Financial Crisis

While some may argue that the UN has been ineffective in resolving global problems, the world has recently experienced an expanded UN role in almost every area of the world. For example, the UN's unprecedented operations within the internal affairs of Iraq to assist the Kurds may be the beginning of a much stronger international organization. However, while the UN is gaining respect, it is also struggling to pay the basic day to day operations. This paradox of expanded UN responsibilities without the necessary financial backing has placed the very survival of the organization in jeopardy.

The financial difficulty the UN is currently experiencing has plagued the organization since its inception. A study conducted in the early 1960's of UN financing reached the conclusion that the constant trend of inadequate funds has always been at a crisis level. The problem

has become so extreme that Secretary General Javier Perez de Cuellar in November 1990 had to borrow money from peacekeeping funds to meet required payments of the regular budget. The Secretary General stressed that the UN's financial situation would continue to be "extremely fragile" so long as its reserves were not fully funded.

History of the Deficit

Since the total annual costs of all UN-related activities amount to a fraction of 1% of the members' military budgets, one may appropriately conclude that financial difficulties should not present a major concern for the organization. However, the history of UN funding problems is extensive. In 1975, the General Assembly created a Special Negotiating Committee on Financial Emergency to address the crisis. While much discussion has taken place, little effective measures have been adopted in order to combat the situation. The underlying reason for inadequate UN funding and inaction toward a reasonable solution is the theme that the organization obtains all its responsibilities or powers from the nation-states. Consequently, the UN receives funds almost exclusively through the contributions of its members.

The UN has been one victim of the Cold War. In the past the superpowers have withheld funds because of disputes over the responsibility of peacekeeping operations and their expenses. North-South debates have driven countries to refuse to contribute on the basis of policy disagreements. However, the financial crisis intensified in 1986 when the U.S. Congress proposed unilateral action to dramatically reduce U.S. contributions to the UN regular budget.

The UN Budget

Several budgets exist within the UN system. The basic budget for operating the administrative machinery and meeting the costs of the major organs and their auxiliary agencies is the regular budget. In 1946, the original budget stood at 20 million dollars. Growing constantly, it reached a level approaching one billion dollars in 1991.

Contributions to the regular budget are assessed among the member states according to a formula based primarily on the state's ability to pay. In 1946, the Committee on Contributions determined the percentage of the total budget to be allotted to each member on the basis of : 1) national income; 2) per capita income; 3) economic dislocations resulting from WWII; and 4) the ability of members to obtain foreign currencies. While the U.S. was originally assessed 39.89% of the UN regular budget, that figure has gradually decreased to 25%

in 1991. The ten largest contributors fund three-fourths of the budget, while 78 member states pay the minimum amount.

The second category of budgets involves special budgets designated by the UN for economic and social programs including the United Nations Children's Fund, the United Nations Development Program, the World Food Program, and the like. The budgets of these programs are funded by voluntary contributions rather than by assessments. While these projects have been extremely dependent on U.S. contributions, constituting 30-80% of these special fund budgets in the past, the levels of U.S. voluntary financial assistance have plummeted to 25% or less in recent years.

The specialized agencies affiliated with the UN through the Economic and Social Council compose another area of UN budgets. Budget assessments are allocated on a scale roughly equivalent to that for the UN regular budget. Many times the budgets of these agencies surpass the levels of the UN regular budget.

UN peacekeeping efforts present the fourth and most controversial category of budgets. The high costs of such operations, as in the Congo in the 1960's, along with the attempt to assess peacekeeping expenses on the basis of UN regular budget assessments, have been the major source of financial difficulties in these UN peace and security efforts. The concept beneath the surface of financing peacekeeping involves the willingness of member states to collectively participate in peace maintenance efforts. For example, the Soviets refused to fund the UN Force for the Congo (ONUC) on the premise that the cost of the operation should be the responsibility of the nations that initiated and caused the problem (e.g., Belgium).

UN Efforts to Finance Peacekeeping Operations

As Ruth Russell argued in 1970, "The UN financial crisis is not ostensibly due to an incapacity of the member states to pay but a result of their unwillingness to do so." But the fact that the UN peacekeeping budget is vastly smaller than the military expenditures of nations, the issue of non-payment was due more to political and legal aspects than financial ones.

This aspect is illustrated by the separate UN peacekeeping efforts of the 1960's in the Congo and the Middle East. After a lengthy debate over the General Assembly's ability to authorize peacekeeping forces, the General Assembly sought an advisory opinion of the ICJ. The court ruled that "the expenses of the organization shall be borne by the members apportioned by the General Assembly." However, General Assembly resolutions and ICJ opinions were insufficient in providing a solution to the UN's financial woes of UN peacekeeping forces in the mid-1960's. As an emergency, the UN was able to issue bonds totalling $200 million as an interim measure to maintain the two UN peacekeeping forces in existence at the time.

The crisis came to a culmination point in 1964 when the Soviet Union and France (which refused to pay the Suez cost) were threatened with deprivation of their votes in the General Assembly under Article 19 which says that UN members "shall have no vote in the General Assembly if the amount of its arrears equals or exceeds the amount of the contributions due from it for the preceding two full years." Although this issue became a critical test of wills in the ongoing cold war, the U.S. backed down and the UN was ultimately left with no new ways to reach permanent financial stability.

Since the 1960's, the UN has experienced consistent financial instability with regard to its peacekeeping forces.

Recent U.S. Contributions to the UN

The UN never recovered from its financial difficulties of the 1960's, and in 1986 and 1987 the U.S. provided a virtual death blow to the organization. The U.S., especially during the Reagan administration, condemned the UN for the anti-Americanism that was believed to have dominated the activities and program of the organization. Many argued that "the place (UN) was long a hotbed of third world radicalism intent on redistributing wealth and power."

Primarily due to the UN focus on third world issues, the U.S. Congress adopted the so-called Kassebaum amendment. The proposal declared that "unless the UN replaced the one-state, one-vote requirement on budgetary questions with weighted voting based on the size of a member's assessed contribution, the U.S. would unilaterally reduce its contributions from 25% to 20% of the regular budget." This action violated the UN Charter in two ways. First, it is a distinct violation of U.S. treaty obligations in the Charter. Moreover, the change in voting procedure required an amendment to the Charter which would have been very difficult to achieve in the short run, if ever.

In 1986, the UN total deficit reached $250 million with the U.S. owing approximately one third of these arrears. Currently, the U.S. delinquent payments total about $600 million. Yet, President Bush has changed the U.S. viewpoint, and he has promised that the U.S. will make full arrears payments by 1994. For the past ten months, the U.S. has paid its 1990-91 assessment, and authorized payment of 1/5th of the arrearage.

UN Authority for Collection

Apart from depriving a state of its right to vote in the General Assembly for non-payment of arrearages, how else can the UN collect back dues from nation states? One proposal is to authorize the Secretary General to sue states in the World Court for arrearage and to impose interest and penalties. This would require an amendment of the court statute and perhaps of the UN Charter, but in the long run, it may be the best route to follow.

Another idea is to enable the Secretary General to go into national courts to collect back dues and to use national judicial procedures to seize assets for non-payment. These ideas may seem unrealistic in a world of sovereign states, but they are necessary elements of a future world order where the U.N. is to be the principal agency for enforcing a world rule of law.

At the very least, there ought to be a way for the UN to assess interest when non-payment is based on policy and not financial hardship considerations. In any event, the question of assessment collection and revenue raising authority must be central to any transformation of the UN into a world federation.

Autonomous Sources of UN Revenue

Although the U.S. has promised to pay its arrears, the UN still must cope with an insufficient budget in a world demanding a greater UN active presence. The first step is to obtain overdue payments from member states, but this is only a portion of what can

be done to improve UN financial solvency. Independent sources of revenue would allow the UN not only to assist a greater number of critical areas around the world, but also to build the necessary global structures to deal with international crises. Only about 3 percent of current revenue comes from such sources as charges for services and sales of publications and stamps, but most proposals for autonomous finances involve greater sums of money. While some of the following ideas for increased revenue may seem radical to some countries, small steps toward independent sources of funding are realistic goals.

International Territories

One of the most popular concepts identified as an independent source of revenue is the ocean and seabeds. The Convention on the Law of the Sea signed in 1982 provides for the development of an international agency to regulate exploitation of the ocean floor under the high seas lying beyond the coastal waters subject to national jurisdiction. While this concept is favored by many, the Convention on the Law of the Sea has not been entered into force. A push in this direction would place a foot in the door for the monitoring and regulation of future exploration sites such as Antarctica and outer space. That first step would be the UN Seabed Authority providing leasing rights to private corporations.

The most complex part of the Law of the Sea Treaty involves deep-sea mining of manganese nodules. An international seabed authority would provide mining concessions and would operate mining operations through a subordinate agency called the "Enterprise." Certain fees and sharing of technology are also involved. Revenues accruing to the Seabed Authority Council are designated for development assistance. The legal barrier to the operation of this Authority is that the needed ratification of the Treaty by 60 member states has not yet been obtained. The key to a successful Authority is not only subject to ratification, but also to ratification by the most powerful countries.

The U.S. refusal to approve the Treaty raises some significant questions. While the U.S. favors some aspects of the Law of the Sea Treaty, it will not be immune from the portions to which it does not affirm. A New World Order should not tolerate a U.S. attempt to impose its own hegemony over international territories such as the high seas.

Multinational Licensing

One of the most controversial items proposed for autonomous UN revenue is the licensing of multinational corporations. The Commission to Study the Organization of Peace has recommended that "such corporations would be subject to special regulations to be adopted by the UN, and the United Nations should have the power to impose reasonable taxes on them, and national taxes on such corporations would be proportionately restricted." The greatest barrier to this concept is the strong influence of multinational companies on international politics. While many proposals have been developed by intergovernmental working groups and discussed at the Commission on Transnational Corporations, real progress toward autonomous revenue of this type is unlikely in the near future.

Other International Fees

Numerous recommendations for other kinds of taxes or licenses have been discussed on the international level, including the following:
1) taxes on international travel or international passport fees;
2) taxes designated for UN funding but collected by member states;
3) surcharges on international mail or global communications (telephone, airline, shipping, etc.);
4) fees for the use of international straits and waterways;
5) "finders fees" for aid in discovering and developing new resources;
6) substantial increase in UN fees for services performed by specialized agencies of the UN;
7) taxes on military transfers or charges on a percent of each nation's national military budget;
8) levies on international trade with revenue devoted to addressing world hunger and poverty.

Pollution Penalties

Another concept that has begun to gain momentum is a penalty for pollution of the global environment. Although this would be a source of revenue, its main purpose is to be punitive in nature. The goal of such a monetary penalty is to stop polluters, not provide a major resource for UN funding. Moreover, such measures would provide the preventative means necessary for the maintenance of our planet.

Voluntary Contributions

Besides the voluntary contributions of the national governments of member states, private donations can also be a source of UN revenue. UNICEF depends on voluntary contributions from both states and individuals for its operation. This type of funding may also be instrumental in providing the UN with finances for its regular budget. This may be especially true if private or foundation contributions can be made with suitable exemptions from national taxation. The bill proposed by former Congressperson John Seiberling needs to be reintroduced. This would allow for individuals to contribute directly to the UN on a tax-deductible basis independent of the U.S. government's annual assessed payment to the UN.

Conclusion

While many argue that independent sources of UN revenue such as taxes on military transfers or mail services take away from a member state's sovereignty, these measures would actually strengthen each nation's ability to protect itself. For example, the funds obtained from international taxes would provide programs such as pollution monitoring and high seas regulations that benefit all.

If President Bush truly seeks to attain a New World Order Under Law, the UN must obtain the necessary funds to support the critical structures for a world ruled by law. Such concepts as an International Criminal Court, improvements in UN verification, UN rapid deployment forces, and the like vitally require the UN to develop and support an expanded budget. While most nations have consistently opposed autonomous revenue actions (President Carter in his 1978 report on UN Reform did support the concept), member states may not have a choice in today's world where one nation cannot possibly attempt to solve crises in every corner of the globe. The recent Persian Gulf crisis illustrates the fact that the UN's role in world affairs is necessary. What needs to be recognized is that the UN must have the financial backing in order to develop and sustain programs targeted at global concerns that also individually serve the nations of our fragile planet.

Discussion Questions

1. Can the UN survive without increased revenue from sources independent of its member states?

2. What authority should the UN be given to collect back dues from member states? Should it have the right to impose interest and penalties?

3. Which concepts of autonomous revenue in your view are most viable in today's world?

4. How can world federalists better inform people about the urgency, not only

of U.S. contributions, but also about the need for a larger UN budget?

5. Many good ideas for autonomous sources of UN financing have been discussed for decades. Through what institution or by what specific means can these theoretical concepts be transformed into practical actions?

6. Should a UN World Federation have the authority to impose and collect taxes from individuals or corporations? If so, what kind of taxes?

REFERENCES AND SUGGESTED READING

Anderson, H. "Getting Some Respect." Newsweek 112:36-7 August 8, 1988.

Bennett, A. Leroy. International Organizations: Principles & Issues. Prentice Hall, New Jersey, 1988.

Crozier, B. "Closing Time for the UN?" National Review 43 (May 13, 1991): 44-45.

Miele, Wayne. U.S. State Department Office of Legislative Affairs. January 1991.

Rife, Roseann. Monograph #3: The Current UN Financial Crisis. The Center for UN Reform Education, 1987.

Russell, Ruth. The General Assembly: Patterns/Problems/Prospects New York, Carnegie Endowment for International Peace, 1970.

Steele, David. The Reform of the UN. England, Chatham Ltd., 1987.

Stoessinger, John. Financing the UN System. Washington, DC, The Brookings Institute, 1964.

UN Documents. UN Charter. UN Statistical Yearbook. Law of the Sea Convention. Status of Contributions to UN Regular Budget. New York.

"UN Financial Situation Still Extremely Fragile." UN Chronicle 28 (March 91): 92.

Part Three
ENVIRONMENT, ECONOMICS, AND HUMAN RIGHTS

11. Global Environment: Should the UN Have More Authority?

by Aram Fuchs

The global environment is being destroyed by man. The problems are no longer only local or regional. Basic resources like air and water--the common inheritance of all humankind--are being affected by processes that are global in scope.

Consciousness of the environment has expanded to include not simply problems crossing contiguous national boundaries, but those problems threatening the planet itself as an integrated ecosystem. For the first time in human history, we are confronted with a single issue that challenges all nations and all people to participate in a unified effort, or risk losing that which sustains us all.

New ways of thinking are beginning to emerge from many national and regional groups which have taken to heart the enormity of the planet's environmental challenges. Many individuals and groups are proposing new ways of doing business that look at the world more holistically. This new attitude can be summed up in the increasingly popular slogan, "think globally, act locally". Although these proposals represent great strides toward the kind of global outlook that will be essential to life in the 21st century, scarcely any thought or effort has yet been put into planning the international institutional structures that are needed to meet the global crisis.

UNEP's Present Role

The creation of an environment program within the United Nations in 1972

From Global Ecology Handbook, published by the Global Tomorrow Coalition, 1990.

represented a great stride forward. In 1991, however, it has become evident that, despite many good works, UNEP (The UN Environmental Program) may lack the political muscle to take on the global environmental challenges of today, such as climate disruption and ozone depletion. The United Nations is undertaking a second major conference on the environment twenty years after Stockholm, in 1992. It is scheduled to take place in Rio de Janeiro, Brazil. Organizations concerned with the environment from around the world are preparing to make this conference a catalyst to reform and strengthen the international institutions to deal with the expanding global threats.

The organization that is charged with dealing with the environmental problems in the United Nations is called the United Nations Environmental Program (UNEP). During the 70's and 80's UNEP concentrated on monitoring the destruction of the world environment and acting as a catalyst to encourage nations to cooperate on regional plans. But now it is necessary to extend the role of UNEP from a mere monitor and catalyst to an active enforcer. If the world is to meet the new global environmental challenges, we cannot rely solely on the hope of cooperation by 160 or 170 independent separate national governments with UNEP acting only as a cheerleader. To maintain UNEP only as an environmental watchdog and cheerleader is a prescription for global disaster.

New Institutional Mechanism

Elliot Richardson, former head of the United States delegation to the Law of the Sea Conference and former three-time Cabinet Secretary, saw this point very clearly. In a perceptive column in the New York Times on 7 February, 1990, he wrote: "Environmentalists and politicians can argue the costs and benefits of international action on global warming from now until doomsday, and they probably will. But nothing will get done without an institutional mechanism to develop, institute and enforce regulations across national boundaries." Twenty-four national leaders also recognized the inadequacy of the 1972 UNEP mandate when on 11 March 1989, they signed what is known as the "Declaration of the Hague". That declaration called for "new institutional authority" within the framework of the United Nations.

The Stockholm Initiative

More recently, thirty-six world leaders including Jimmy Carter, Vaclev Havel and Eduard Shevardnadzie signed a document called "The Stockholm Initiative". The Initiative is a document calling for an enhanced world authority that would have the power to attack the world's problems aggressively, including the environment. The document declares, "few issues accentuate the interdependence of nations as the environmental problems." Environmental destruction does not abide by political boundaries. A river polluted in one country flows towards others. Fossil fuels burned into the air in Ohio come down in the form of acid rain in Canada.

Ironically, the current destruction of our environment actually provides a unique opportunity for the world's national governments to form a closer bond. In September 1987, most industrialized nations signed the Montreal Protocol which provided for a 50% reduction in the production and use of halon and chlorofluorocarbons and other ozone-depleting chemicals. In order to facilitate developing countries to sign the Protocol (only 13 signed) the signers included a fund that the developing countries could use to aid in their transfer to safer chemicals. On June 29, 1990 in London ninety-three nations agreed to speed up the process by calling for a halt in CFC production by the end of the century. China and India, which did not sign the Montreal document, agreed to sign the more stringent London document. The London Amendment gave poorer nations ten more years after 1999 to reach the goal.

The World's Federalists have long concerned themselves with the international institutional dimensions of the environment issue. The first World Federalist pamphlet that dealt with the planetary environment was published in 1972, the same year as the Stockholm conference.

On July 14, 1990, the Council of the World Federalist Movement, representing twenty national branches of the movement, adopted an environmental policy calling for the adoption of a Law of the Atmosphere and for new UN institutional authority.

Law of the Atmosphere

The principles for a Law of the Atmosphere and the similar Law of the Sea is that they should be both declared a "global commons". The law would pool the sovereignty that all nations claim over the atmosphere and the high seas into one grouping. Any violation of that sovereignty would be punished by the entire group, just as any violations of national sovereignty are defended.

In a background paper called, "A Law of the Atmosphere", Fergus Watt, a Canadian World Federalist, describes a general obligation of states to protect and preserve the atmosphere. Although many delegates to a recent international experts' meeting recommend inclusion of this principle in a framework umbrella convention on protection of the atmosphere, there is not unanimous agreement among the experts on the need for such a provision. Any such general obligation would imply that states are liable and accountable if they do not "protect and preserve the atmosphere." But the nations must be held liable to any abuse of the atmosphere or similar violation of the sea or else it will continue unabated. An international environmental organization is needed to keep the nations in check.

Enforcement Measures and Incentives

World Federalists contend that the 1992 convention should create a new UN institutional authority that has the power to make decisions binding on all nations. Without such power some nations will continue to pollute the global commons. One important function of a new UN institutional authority should be "to adopt regulations for protection of the international environment, as well as guidelines and regulations interpreting and applying environmental treaties." While treaties can paint with broad strokes the actions needed, applying guidelines to specific situations needs constant monitoring. Such enforcement measures might as a last resort include the imposition of economic sanctions and also levying fines on offenders, whether they be individuals, corporations or governments. While enforcement should be the primary responsibility of states that are parties to the agreement, there must be recourse to an international interpreting and enforcing body with powers to issue orders to "cease and desist."

Incentives are also a tool to enforce such environmental treaties. A prototype provision is found in the Treaty on the Ozone which requires nations not to trade chemicals with nations which are not signatories. With this provision, the signers of a particular environmental treaty become a type of trading bloc, with all others excluded from this potentially valuable asset.

Trade policies should not only yield rewards for treaty adherence but trade policies are key to insuring the success of sustainable technologies. Costs on the world market need to reflect the environmental costs of products over their entire life-cycle; protectionism often undermines sustainability.

Other incentives might include generous technology transfers, large amounts of additional development aid, and debt forgiveness for treaty adherents. By creating an adequate system of incentives to bring nations into the treaty regime-- fostering awareness of the clear and imminent dangers of environmental inaction, supplemented by generous financial and trade advantages for signatories--treaty enforcement could be made much less difficult.

The signers of The Stockholm Initiative declared that the "political will to halt the tide of environmental destruction must be mobilized." The United Nations Conference on the Environment and Development (UNCED) to be held in 1992 must be a "breakthrough for achieving sustainable development."

CAPE Proposals

The World needs a strong international body willing and having the capabilities to govern the international community in their environmental affairs. The Consortium for Action to Protect the Earth (CAPE), a group of six American environmental groups, has published what they believe are the most pressing changes needed for the United Nations to be successful in protecting the world's heritage. The six in the consortium are The Environmental Defense Fund, Friends of the Earth, National Audubon Society, National Wildlife Federation, Natural Resources Defense Council and the Sierra Club.

The first and possibly most important is for the UN environmental organization to have the power to set environmental standards that all countries and businesses must follow. By creating the proverbial "level playing field", the international organization will reduce the incentive to abuse the environment under the context of competition. The organization must have a constitution "enabling it to establish such standards by majority vote decision-making procedures and to act more rapidly and effectively to address environmental problems." The new organization proposed by CAPE would be similar to the International Labor Organization (ILO) in form and function. The ILO has been very efficient in creating worldwide standards of acceptable rules in the workplace. The UN environmental organization must achieve similar success in creating environmental standards.

Another major proposal of CAPE, which World Federalists have long agreed upon, is to expand international adjudication of environmental treaties signed by nations. World Federalists advocate a special arbitral tribunal to adjudicate environmental disputes. The capacity of such tribunals and of the International Court of Justice should be expanded to allow individuals to seek redress for violations of international law.

World Bank's Myopic Financing

At this time of environmental crisis some international agencies have actually advanced environmental destruction throughout the world. The World Bank led the way in financing Brazil's road building plan into the Amazon. Their arguments were morally sound. The Amazon basin was a natural resource that if exploited could raise the standard of living of Brazilian peasants. But the Bank ignored the supplemental long term environmental costs to the world. The destruction to the basin and subsequent burning of the forest's wood has increased the carbon dioxide in the atmosphere. This has increased the impact of the greenhouse effect. The destruction of the millions of hectares of forest and pollution of the water has led to the extinction of thousands of species. The World Bank was incredibly myopic in its financing of the Brazilian plan. But it is not entirely the Bank's fault. There needs to be an institutional check against such internationally induced environmental destruction. All international development agencies should be required to prepare environmental impact statements for all of their projects. The World needs to link environmental protection with economic development. Maurice Strong, the UNCED Secretary-General, supports the creation of an agency that will have the responsibility of auditing all UN actions in environment terms.

Methods of Financing

The last aspect that needs to be discussed is the method of financing the projects needed to halt the environmental destruction. A recent poll of 1,000 American adults found that 83% were in favor of an international arms sales tax administered by the United Nations. While the tax might be difficult to collect initially, it could, if collected from the exporter, be a significant disincentive. A tax on future production of nuclear weapons would make a great deal of sense. The nuclear waste resulting from such production has been a source of great environmental danger. The Brandt Commission summed up the political difficulties in getting agreement on international taxes but concluded that the arguments in favor of such taxation were "very powerful."

A tax on fossil fuel consumption would have a direct relationship to the greenhouse effect in that it would aid in the reduction of the major portion of the greenhouse gases threatening the planet. The international fossil fuel tax is most likely the best all-around alternative for obtaining an autonomous source of funding. Our fossil fuel consumption has been made particularly extravagant by hidden subsidies to the fossil fuel industry. The tax would essentially pay for the environmental damage that the industry now causes but does not have the obligation to reimburse for. Experts agree that a fossil fuel tax would be a simple and effective means to expedite a switch to more efficient energy usage and give renewable energy the level playing field it deserves.

Going into 1992, the time is ripe to push for an international fossil fuel or carbon emissions tax, with all, or at least a portion, of the proceeds going to a Global

Environmental Fund. The concept of licensing the global commons is already incorporated into the Law of the Sea Treaty. The UN maintains the rights to seabed minerals because they lie within the deep seabed area designated as the global commons. The UN retains the right under the treaty to charge licensing fees from would-be miners. This licensing principle could and should be applied to Antarctica, and geostationary communication satellite parking as suggested by the Brundtland Commission.

The Ethics of Survival

The environment is under attack. Man, through his genius, has found ways to dominate mother earth. It is only his morality that can save it. The Stockholm Initiative says, "What value should we place on our genius if unconstrained by ethics of survival, it leads the human race to despoil its earthly habitation?" We are at a time of crisis like never before. A code of survival is needed if we are to continue the standard of living that we have now attained. The code must be international in scope and strict in language. The United Nations is the perfect body to institute such codes. The UN must be given the authority to issue environmental regulations that can be arbitrated in an environmental tribunal.

The environment is our common heritage. It is the place from which all of our wealth is derived. In the past few years we have seen the signs of awesome destruction. There is a hole in the atmosphere over Antarctica. There are massive droughts in California. Eastern Europe is barely livable. These problems are due to the laxity of all national governments. To end the destruction, an organization is needed that has an international constituency. This organization is the United Nations.

Discussion Questions

1. Should industrialized nations be obligated to pay to upgrade a developing nation's industries to a cleaner level?

2. Which is a greater national security threat: the USSR or damage to the environment?

3. Do you think the current loss to our biodiversity is just a clear cut example of Darwin's theory of "survival of the fittest"?

4. Is it arrogant for richer nations to demand that poorer nations stop exploiting their natural resources even though rich nations have done that themselves for the past 150 years?

5. Do you believe global warming is actually happening? If not, do you still believe we should reduce use of greenhouse inducing gases?

6. Are you willing to pay much more for a product that is environmentally sound compared to paying less for one that is environmentally destructive?

REFERENCES AND SUGGESTED READINGS

Fornos, Werner. **The Fault of Our Forest: The Human Element.** The Population Institute, 1990.

Leonard, Pamela and Hoffmann, Walter. **Effective Global Environmental Protection: World Federalist Proposals to Strengthen the Role of the United Nations.** October 1990.

On the Fate of the Earth. Transcripts of Washington, D.C. Conference. Earth Island Institute, 1985.

Shea, Cynthia Pollock. **"Protecting Life on Earth: Steps to Save the Ozone Layer."** Worldwatch Paper 87. Washington, D.C.

State of the Environment: 1991. United Nations Environmental Program, 1991.

12. Population: What Can the UN Do?

by Aram Fuchs

The population of the world is still exploding. Presently, it is at 5.4 billion. By 2025, the "most likely" projections have population overflowing at over 8.5 billion people. In 1974, population was only four billion people. These numbers become even more frightening when we realize that 90% of that growth will occur in the impoverished third world. Population control is a necessary element in the fight for providing the present world's population with an improved quality of life. Lester Brown said in this book, In the Human Interest, "If we define optimum population as a level by which further increases would no longer improve the quality of human life, then world population has already passed the optimum level." This declining quality of life is leading to battles over the available resources left. Recent events in the news show the need to reduce the demand of dwindling resources. The War in the Gulf was unquestionably over the control of one of the more important natural resources, oil. The Ethiopian Civil War created massive famines that required massive international support. The needs of ever expanding population in Brazil helped to force its government to open the Amazon and its surrounding land for exploitation. Subsequent deforestation has accelerated the greenhouse effect. It has also decimated local native peoples with western diseases.

The population explosion has affected every arena of human interaction. "Physical growth," says Dennis Meadows, Director of the Institute for Policy and Social Science Research at the University of New Hampshire, "is the common factor in practically every significant problem facing the planet, and these problems cannot be solved without addressing the limits to growth." Economically, population growth has caused a sharp decline in the quality of life, especially in the Third World. Politically, it has helped bring diplomatic conflicts to the brink of war. Ecologically, it has necessitated the rape and destruction of the earth at the expense of the other species that share the earth with us and future generations of human beings. Family planning is needed now.

How UNFPA Slows Population Growth

The United Nation's involvement in population control began with the birth of its charter. In 1946, the United Nations Population Commission was established. It focused mainly as a data-gathering organization. It encouraged member nations to undertake national censuses so nations could begin to understand the rate at which their populations were actually growing. For the next twenty years, there were several acknowledgements of the consequences of overpopulation by other United Nations organizations. There were two purely technical conferences on the subject of population control. The first was in 1954 in Rome. The second was in Belgrade in 1964.

As the world's population continued to expand, the United Nations began to devote more resources to the problem. In 1967 a fund that would eventually become the United Nations Population Fund (UNFPA) was established as a segment of the Secretary-General's Trust Fund. The

Figure 3.1
World Population Growth, 1 A.D. to 2100

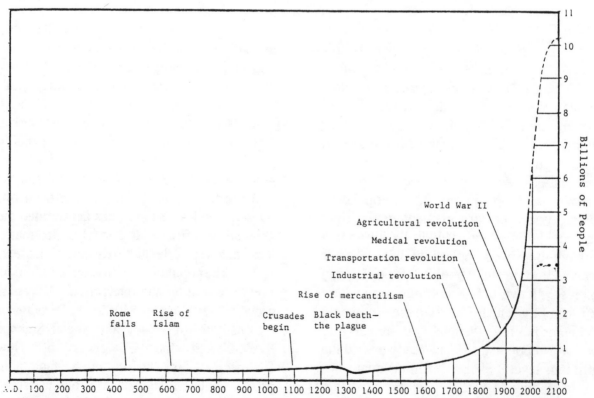

World Population Growth, 1 A.D. to 2100. From Global Ecology Handbook, Global Tomorrow Coalition, 1990.

government of Denmark was the first national government to contribute to the fund with a donation of $100,000. In 1969, the fund was given its independence as a separate entity. Five years later it had a budget of $175 million.

In that year, 1974, an international conference on population was held in Bucharest. This was the first UN sponsored conference on population aimed at political delegates, not scientific technicians. The conference was wrought with debate between the industrialized nations, which wanted to donate money to establish an international population control fund, and the unreceptive developing nations. The potential donors tried to convince developing nations of the impending doom caused by the population explosion. They tried rational arguments using data, graphs and charts. But the developing nations were not receptive. They perceived the idea of "population control" as another scheme by which industrialized nations would maintain a quasi-colonial control over them. Out of this fiery debate, Rafael Salas, then the Executive-Director of UNFPA, somehow managed to formulate a consensus that would be known as the World Population Plan of Action. This statement confirmed the legitimacy of international population activities. But at the same time it allowed nations to retain sovereignty in completing their own plans for action to attack the problem. UNFPA's unwillingness to allow increased intrusion into a country's sovereignty is the limitation that may make the United Nations' role in population control seem modest at best.

Population control is a very controversial issue. Various ethnic and religious groups around the world have widely diverging views on the subject. Religion still plays a major role for millions of people, especially in developing countries. Recently, a group of Islamic religious leaders meeting in Indonesia agreed that there was "a need for accessible family planning." Amazingly, they even deemed it acceptable for Islamic men to be voluntarily sterilized. The global populace is gradually realizing the need to control its population. In heavily catholicized Latin America, only 57% of the couples that want access to birth control can receive it. Distribution channels simply are not filled with the modern contraceptives that are wanted by consumers.

UNFPA's main method of helping to stabilize the world's population is simple, providing reliable condoms and other modern contraceptives to those that want it, but cannot afford it. The following chart illustrates the potential success of improving distribution channels to satisfy this need.

Percentage of couples that want birth control and have it.

In Africa   25%
In Asia   43%
In Latin America   57%

The UN's goal is to increase the number of couples in developing countries using birth control from 381 million to 567 million by the end of the century, a net increase of over fifty percent. This target would raise the proportion of married women using modern, reliable contraceptives from 51% to 59%. Even if this ambitious goal is achieved, UNFPA has already conceded that the global population will rise to at least 6.4 billion people by the year 2001.

UNFPA has been very creative in trying to extend the distribution channels of modern contraceptives. One method is using distribution channels that are already in place for other products. In Nigeria, women selling products in markets are given a 25 percent commission on sales of modern contraceptives. In Thailand, even the poor will spend money for contraceptives for sale in convenient shops instead of out-of-the-way clinics. An experiment was run in the Ogun State of Nigeria. A population organization shipped the same condom in two different lots. The first lot was given a brand name and an advertising campaign complete with a jingle sung by a famous Nigerian pop star. The other lot remained a generic brand and was sold through pharmacists and chemists. The brand name condom outsold the generic 2.5:1!

A New Crisis: U.S. Withdrawal from Population Control Efforts

With UNFPA's programs beginning to make some headway into the population problems, the fourth international conference on population was held in 1984 at Mexico City. As a symbol of the importance that UNFPA had attained in the fight for population control, the Executive Director of UNFPA, Rafael Salas, was named Secretary-General of the conference. By 1984 the developing nations were beginning to experience the full horrors of overpopulation. The small growth in G.N.P. that they had managed in the last ten years was overwhelmed by the massive growth in their populations. They came to the conference ready to commit to an aggressive plan of action. In a strange twist of irony, the United States switched its position. The United States' delegate maintained a position at Mexico City that population growth was only a "neutral" factor in Third World development. The

United States claimed that the free market, by increasing the developing nations' G.N.P., would eliminate the ills of overpopulation. The other delegates were amazed. But they did not stand by and watch the population control movement crumble at the hands of its original leadership. The other nations of the world grasped the reins of leadership from the U.S. and produced 88 amendments to the plan produced at the Bucharest conference.

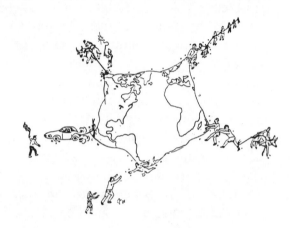

*From Global Ecology Handbook,
Global Tomorrow Coalition, 1990.*

In 1985, under pressure from a conservative constituency, the U.S. began to withdraw its funding from UNFPA. In August of 1986 it completely canceled it. The Reagan administration rationalized the cancellation by claiming that UNFPA "co-managed" the population control plan in China which allegedly had "coerced abortions" as part of its plan to limit its population. The administration argued that under the Kemp-Inuoye amendment to the foreign aid bill of 1985, the government was obligated to deny funding "to any country or organization that supports or participates in the management of a program of coercive abortion or involuntary sterilization."

The argument that UNFPA "co-manages" the Chinese population control program is ludicrous. UNFPA donates ten million dollars to the program. The total budget for the Chinese program is over one billion dollars. That is less than 1% of the entire budget! UNFPA has a staff in China of four people, while the overall plan employs 160,000. The aggressive nature of the Chinese population control program brings up interesting ethical questions. Does any governmental agency have the right to limit a citizen's right to bear children? It could be argued that government does have the right to this limitation when population growth reaches the point of interfering with the government's obligation to protect the health and economic welfare of its citizens and the ecological integrity of its land. Perhaps government must be allowed to balance the right to procreate with the obligation to maintain sustainable development.

UNFPA's stated policy "does not provide support, nor has it ever provided support, for abortions or abortion-related activities anywhere in the world." But, nevertheless, in February of 1990, AID announced for the fifth year in a row that the United States would not donate any money to UNFPA.

World Population Limitation Depends on Money

After the withdrawal of aid from the United States, the other major donors agreed to increase their donations. Japan is now the leading donor to UNFPA. It contributes 22% of the budget. The other major donors are, in order of the amount of donations: Germany, Netherlands, Norway, Sweden, Finland, Denmark, Canada, United Kingdom, Switzerland and Italy. UNFPA now gives out a total of 1/3 of all population control and family planning aid worldwide. It is known as one of the more efficient and respected UN institutions. It is one of the few that has set criteria in order to distribute its money more efficiently. In 1991, the criteria have been established as follows:

1. National income
2. Average family size
3. Population growth rate
4. Infant mortality level
5. Rural population density
6. Literacy among women

Fifty-six countries are now eligible for prioritized UNFPA funding based on the above criteria. Thirty-one of these countries are in Africa. UNFPA distributes 70% of its available funding to priority countries. By 1993, its goal is to increase that number to 80%.

In order to further strengthen its ability to attack the problem, UNFPA has also established a generalized list of factors that influence family size around the world. UNFPA believes that no one factor is more important than another. They tend to reinforce each other.

The five factors are:
1. Women's status in society
2. Maternal and child health care
3. Information and access to family planning
4. Family income
5. Level of education of women

In 1989, another international conference on population was convened. Seventy-nine delegates from around the world met in Amsterdam. The conference was entitled, "A Better Life for Future Generations." The delegates of the conference, which was organized by UNFPA in coordination with the government of the Netherlands, essentially held a forum to legitimize UNFPA's goals by having them approved by an international consensus. The Amsterdam Declaration was signed by all of the attending delegates. It declared that the worldwide population control budget must reach nine billion dollars. An annual increase of 7 percent is needed to reach that figure by the end of the century. Nafis Sadik, the current Executive Director of UNFPA, claims that her organization will need $500 million by 1994 and one billion dollars by the turn of the century. That will only be 11% of the money that will be needed for population control worldwide. UNFPA recommends obtaining the whole of this money in the following way:

> 1.0 billion dollars from UNFPA
>
> 3.5 billion dollars from other international organizations
>
> 3.5 billion dollars from national governments
>
> 1.0 billion dollars from consumers in developing countries
>
> 9.0 billion dollars

As sociologists have long known, the degree of affluence in a society is a factor in population control. As material welfare increases, families tend automatically to limit their size. Therefore, the larger challenge of the UN's population control effort is to raise the standard of living worldwide.

Nevertheless, the United Nations can advance the cause of population control with very little expansion of its powers. Population management is a popular cause in most parts of the world. UNFPA has received donations from over 144 nations representing every ideological and moral cause. UNFPA, under the leadership of Rafael Salas, created an almost complete world consensus from an international arena that at first seemed not to want to listen. Recently, Nafis Sadik has created an agenda to set UNFPA ready for the twenty-first century. The agenda requires money. UNFPA must reach its goal of reaching one billion dollars in its budget. With that money, it will be able to further expand its programs and, more importantly, gain more influence to spread its message. The key bottleneck in the world of population control is the large percentage of people that want access to family planning and modern contraceptives and cannot obtain it. Those that need it the most are those that can afford it the least. UNFPA and the world as a whole are obligated to give it to them. The main challenge for UNFPA is raising the money to reach those people. It is that simple.

Discussion Questions

1. Do we, as the current generation, have the ethical right to take away the right to life of others just to maintain our quality of life?

2. Should UNFPA be made part of the required budget of all member nations?

3. Should the United Nations have the right to limit national sovereignty in order to deal with the population explosion?

4. How can the international community, including the United Nations, convince skeptical couples about the need for family planning?

5. What can you do to solve this problem?

REFERENCES AND SUGGESTED READINGS

Brown, Lester. **Building a Sustainable Society**. W. W. Norton & Company, New York, 1981.

Fornos, Werner. **The Remarkable Journey: Two Decades of UNFPA Leadership**. The Population Institute, Washington, D.C., 1989.

Global Tomorrow Coalition. **The Global Ecology Handbook**. Beacon Press, Boston, 1990.

Sadik, Nafis. **The State of World Population 1991**. United Nations Population Fund, New York, 1991.

13. Development: Are New Institutions Needed?

by Anthony Allen

Disparities between the North and South have grown over the four decade life of the UN. The decade of the eighties was particularly difficult for the developing countries. Per capita income and investment in the Lesser Developed Countries (LDCs) fell while the debt burden piled more stress on weak economies. Three fourths of the human family now lives in LDCs, and their poor conditions contribute to many global crises including wars (civil and international), refugees, environmental degradation, and disease. The issue of development therefore must be seen as a security crisis facing the whole world. There is much hope that the LDCs can overcome these problems and become active participants in the world economy. On the whole, LDCs have been economically growing at a more rapid pace than that experienced by industrialized countries. Where countries have been able to develop effective development policies there has been strong development. Development is possible, and the UN is the most logical organization to play a strong role in stimulating LDCs' participation in the world economy because the UN like no other organization contains nearly all nations in its membership.

The UN's role in multilateral technical and financial assistance has grown greatly over the years, but unfortunately it hasn't expanded in a coordinated manner with a single plan. There are three groups of UN economic institutions: the financial organizations, the functional or technical organizations, and the overall competence organizations. As new priorities arose, many new agencies were created, each with its own governing body and directors. This complexity, accompanied with different views of the best way to foster development between the industrialized North and the developing South, adds to the lack of coordination and cohesion in the UN's efforts to assist LDCs. The industrialized West complains about political onesidedness and procedural abuses of UN agencies, while the South criticizes the UN's failure to provide representation and authority in responding to the LDCs' needs. On any given day, as many as fifteen U N organizations may be simultaneously working in a single country organizing separate projects with little or no coordination among themselves. The following list of some of the UN agencies assisting developing nations gives one an idea of this complexity:

Drought victims in Ethiopia, 1984. UN photo 164623.

A. Functional, Technical and Overall Competency Organizations

1. UNDP (United Nations Development Program)

2. UNESCO (UN Educational, Scientific and Cultural Organization)

3. UNITAR (UN Institute for Training and Research)

4. UNIDO (United Nations Industrial Development Organization)

5. ILO (International Labor Organization)

6. FAO (Food and Agricultural Organization)

7. IFAD (International Fund for Agricultural Development)

8. WHO (World Health Organization)

9 UNEP (UN Environment Program)

B. Financial Institutions

1. IBRD (World Bank, International Bank for Reconstruction and Development)

2. IMF (International Monetary Fund)

3. GATT (General Agreement on Trade and Tariffs)

This complex system needs to be better organized if the UN is to play a vitally needed role in stimulating the world economy to benefit rich and poor nations alike. There have been a number of studies which critique the UN economic institutions. This paper will review what major studies have concluded about the need to reform the UN's economic institutions and will raise questions about what type of economic institutions are needed to build a just new world order.

The Failure of the Kassum Report

In 1975 Al Noor Kassum of Tanzania chaired a group of 25 experts appointed by then Secretary General Kurt Waldheim to make specific recommendations to the General Assembly about UN reform. The report began by stating the problem with the UN's uncoordinated economic institutions this way: "It must be recognized that the system is more a product of historical circumstances than of a rational design." The report then recommended eight correction measures:

1. Creation of a new post of Director-General for Development and International Economic Cooperation, which would be second in line to the Secretary General.

2. Consolidation of all special purpose UN funds for pre-investment activity into a single UN Development Authority to be headed by one administrator who would be one of two deputies to the

new Director General for Development and International Economic Cooperation.

3. The reorganization of the Department of Economic and Social Affairs under a second deputy to the Director General, with this department assigned to carry out high level research and planning for the Economic and Social Council and entire UN system.

4. The revitalization of the Economic and Social Council through extensive changes in functions and methods of work.

5. Gradual replacement of the UN Conference on Trade and Development (UNCTAD) with a new comprehensive international trade organization.

6. Retention of the Second Committee (Economic and Financial) of the General Assembly as the committee on international development and economic cooperation and the transfer to it of certain social items now handled by the Third Committee (Social Humanitarian and Cultural).

7. Abolition of the governing council of the UN Environment Program, its role in administering the Environment Fund to be taken over by the Operations Board of UNDA.

8. Creation of a unified employment system for the UN, based upon efficiency, competency and integrity, under which hiring would be done not through politics, but rather through competitive exams.

An Ad Hoc Committee of the General Assembly reviewed the report for two years and reported its findings to the General Assembly in 1978. The General Assembly rejected every proposal except the proposal for a Director General for Development and Economic Cooperation. This post was created but given no real authority. Therefore, the economic institutions of the UN remained in their disjointed condition. The rejection of the Kassum Report by the General Assembly showed that most UN members were not prepared for major UN reform. As Ronald Meltzer concluded in his 1983 book on the UN, The U.S. and the UN Management of Global Change, ". . . the best way to change the UN is to work for incremental change where consensus is possible."

Other Attempts to Streamline UN Structure

Ten years later another report analyzing the shortcomings of the UN's complex system was prepared by Maurice Bertrand. This report looked more broadly at not just the possible cures for the UN problems, but also at the causes of its disfunction. Bertrand's underlying theme was that the object of the UN should not be to foster joint action by members, but should be to negotiate consensus concerning what joint action is possible. Bertrand saw the decentralized and fragmented structures of the UN system as not being suited to the problems of development. The report proposed restructuring the UN into an Economic United Nations where economic problems would take priority over political problems. The structure of such an Economic UN, Bertrand believed, should not be the usual secretariat Assembly Council scheme, but be based on the Ministries Commission set-up now used by the EEC. This arrangement facilitates joint ventures by all members or just a few members of this organization. Bertrand also calls for each delegation to include economic experts side by side with politicians. Bertrand's holistic approach is appealing, but it is obvious that not all problems facing our world and the UN can be solved by

insistence upon negotiating a consensus first and acting later.

In 1990 two distinguished UN experts wrote another report on UN reform. Brian Urquhart, who worked with all five Secretaries General, and Erskine Childers, former senior advisor to the UN Director for Development and International Economic Cooperation, focused completely on leadership of the UN in their report entitled, "A World in Search of Leadership." They both believe that with improved leadership the UN can cope with its urgent agenda.

Regarding the Secretary General's position, they contend that the scope of the job has increased so greatly that no single person can accomplish it. They suggest creating three deputies to the Secretary General to assist in the following areas:

--peace and security with emphasis on peacekeeping

--economic and social matters with emphasis on sustainable development

--administration and management

--public relations, with special attention to cultural diversity

They also stress the need for a more depoliticized and organized process for selecting future Secretary Generals. Specifically, they call for agreed upon rules for nominating, the cessation of individual

campaigning by countries, and making the term of office a single seven-year term.

The report also makes recommendations on improving the way specialized agencies are run. North-South tensions and a frequent lack of quality candidates has stood in the way of strong leadership in the specialized agency realm. Urquhart and Childers conclude that success depends on leadership of all UN organs working together for the same goals. They call for the search process for leadership to be more thorough and for all regions to agree to search for the best candidates based on consensus to depoliticize the process and help the UN utilize sound management practices for better coordination and effectiveness.

During the 1980's there were four major independent commissions that focused on global crises: the North-South Commission, the Independent Commission on Disarmament and Security, the World Commission on Environment and Development and the South Commission. Willy Brandt brought the leaders of each commission together to review the 1980's and outline prospects for the 90's. In April of 1991 these leaders put together the Stockholm Initiative on Global Security and Governance to assess the new opportunities and suggest major areas for multilateral action on global problems.

Regarding development, the Initiative emphasizes the need for all UN development efforts to focus on people-oriented growth strategies. It calls for all UN agencies and the World Community to set targets for the year 2000 including: primary education for all children, equal participation of boys and girls in school, reduction of child mortality by a third and reduction of maternal mortality by half. The Initiative also urges

the UN to put sustainable development high on the agenda of the Security Council.

The Campaign for UN Reform, legislative wing of the U.S. World Federalist Movement, has developed several general proposals for reforming UN economic institutions. Regarding the technical and general competency institutions, the CUNR calls for the creation of an Economic Security Council reorganized out of the current UN Economic and Social Council. This body would: a) Coordinate international development programs with monetary stabilization and trade programs; b) Coordinate UN development programs with the UN Environment Program; c) Assist nations with economic conversion to non-military economies; and d) Support the role of women in development.

UN Financial Institutions

The world economic environment has a huge impact on development. The 1980's witnessed a worsening economic environment for developing countries. Protectionism, falling commodity prices, fluctuating exchange rates and high interest rates were all part of an international economic environment largely shaped outside the influence of the developing countries. The results have been a frightening debt crisis, reduction in net capital flows to the developing world, and a stagnation in aid levels.

The Global Community has become increasingly interdependent. Creation of more equitable monetary and trade programs lags while protectionism and abrupt shifts of private or public capital threaten world economic stability. The UN system's financial organizations played a role in providing a framework for monetary and trade relations as well as granting development loans. The three organizations that will be focused on here are the IMF, World Bank and GATT. The IMF and World Bank were developed out of the conference held by 44 members of the UN in Bretton Woods, NH in 1944. The conference was called to formulate proposals for an International Monetary Fund, but the issue of creating an international Bank for Reconstruction and Development was brought onto the agenda by many developing countries. GATT was founded much later as an international trade organization.

The IMF was established to stabilize monetary conditions, and the World Bank was created to lend capital for productive purposes to stimulate economic growth in borrowing countries. Over the years the definition of each of these organizations has been expanded. The IMF, although not designed originally to focus on developing countries, has had to give special attention to their monetary problems. One new role of the IMF has been to serve as a domestic economic monitor of debt-burdened countries to help them handle debt-servicing. The Bank too has changed. It has moved from narrow banking confined to infrastructure projects to emphasis on basic human needs and income redistribution.

In 1947 fifty-three UN members convened a conference in Havana, Cuba, to organize an international trade organization. The IMF and World Bank were not designed to handle the complex trade issues of stabilization of raw materials prices, commodity prices, cartels and restrictive business practices. The Havana Charter proposed an International Trade Organization to govern trade barriers and contained a section on economic development and reconstruction discussing

the need to regulate international private investment. The U.S. and other industrialized nations perceived such an organization as a threat to free trade. The result was the establishment of the General Agreement on Trade and Tariffs as a limited substitute to the ITO. GATT allows less specifically favorable terms for LDCs. The basic question whether there should be different trade rules for different stages of development has remained an important issue that the UN institutions have not resolved.

All three of these organizations have received much criticism. The World Bank is seen by some as counterproductive to development, and accused of supporting dictators and reactionary elites in the developing world. Others see the Bank as too lax in lending, promoting socialism, and undermining free trade. The IMF has been criticized as failing to give developing countries a voice in shaping international monetary policy. LDCs make up a bulk of the IMF's membership, but continue to lack clout in the IMF because the decision-making process is based primarily on capital contributions to IMF. In 1980 the UN sponsored a conference in Tanzania on International Money and Finance. The delegates called for a new monetary system that gives more attention to developing a monetary policy conducive to LDC development.

GATT vs. UNCTAD

GATT has also received much criticism. In 1965 the UN Conference on Trade and Development was created and the LDC majority of the General Assembly contended that GATT imposes overly burdensome restrictions. UNCTAD called for the application of the rule of law, but emphasized the recognition of differences in the degree of development and in economic and social systems. In 1974 the LDC majority of the General Assembly put forward the Declaration for a New International Economic Order charter on Economic Rights and Duties of States with calls for special treatment of LDCs in trade and economic matters. In 1986 the Uruguay Round was launched as a multi-year GATT trade negotiation. It is the biggest and most ambitious effort to improve GATT's work to create a more stable and predictable system of trade involving over 100 countries.

The calls for change in the international economy have not been received well by the developed nations. The conflict between the North and South on development issues has made the General Assembly mainly a forum for rhetoric with few practical results. Another result of this conflict is that the World Bank, IMF and particularly the GATT are often bypassed by nations and many multinational corporations resulting in an even more unfriendly world economy for poorer nations.

The Stockholm Initiative makes a number of suggestions to improve the international financial situation. The proposals regarding trade, financial flows, debt reduction and development cooperation include:

1. Strengthening of the multilateral framework of trade-related agreements, reducing protectionism on all fronts, and expanding opportunities for developing countries' participation in world trade.

2. A strengthened debt strategy, introducing a strong element of debt forgiveness to radically cut the debt burden, including:

--rescheduling that goes beyond today's by providing relief and applying to a broader range of countries.

--commercial debt restructuring that better corresponds to the secondary market value of that debt.

--increased financing on appropriate terms by the international financial institutions.

3. That all industrialized nations set public time-targets to provide one percent of their GNP for international development cooperation.

The Campaign for UN Reform has called for UNCTAD and the IMF to be given more authority to establish a cohesive and equitable monetary and trading system. The Campaign also recommends:

--An International Trade Organization to resolve tariff disputes.

--An International Common Fund to moderate commodity prices.

--Implementation of UNCTAD proposals to make world trading systems more responsive to LDC's needs.

--Development of regional monetary networks and a centralized international credit reserve system as a step toward an international currency.

--Development of guidelines for the conduct of multinational corporations in host countries.

Concluding Remarks

The complexity of UN economic institutions is matched only by the confusion one can feel after reading the many ideas for how to improve the UN. The studies reviewed in this paper raise three forms of reform ideas. Some of the studies call for the creation of new institutions such as an International Trade Organization and a UN Development Authority. Other proposals, such as the Urquhart and Childers report, call only for readjusting the current UN system without major changes. Still others call for a redefinition of the goals and focus of UN economic institutions. For example, the Bertrand report and the Stockholm Initiative urge that the whole UN system rethink and refocus its energies on building consensus on development issues and making sure the UN's work is always people-oriented. The ideas in all these reports are not mutually exclusive. A just new world order will require the UN to change in many ways both institutionally and philosophically.

Discussion Questions

1. Should the UN consolidate many of its specialized agencies into a UN Development Authority?

2. During the Uruguay Rounds, should the UN transform GATT into an International Trade Organization, or focus its attention on gradually reforming GATT?

3. How can the UN better foster consensus building between the Industrialized North and the Developing South on international economic issues?

4. Should the UN transform the Economic and Social Council into an Economic Security Council to execute important development initiatives and insure that development projects are people-oriented and support the role of women in development?

REFERENCES AND SUGGESTED READINGS

Ashby, L. **UN's Economic Institutions and the Need for Restructuring.** Draft prepared for Center for UN Reform Education, Washington, D.C., 1988.

Bertrand, M. **Joint Inspection Unit Report,** "Some Reflections on Reform of the UN," 1985.

Fourteen Points. Campaign for UN Reform, Washington, D.C., 1988.

Meltzer, R. **The US, the UN and the Management of Global Change.** New York University Press, NY, 1983.

Stockholm Initiative on Global Security and Governance, Prime Minister's Office, Stockholm, Sweden, April 22, 1991.

Urquhart, B. and Childers, E., **A World in Need of Leadership, Tomorrow's UN.** Dag Hammarskjold Foundation, Uppsala, Sweden, 1990.

World Economy, UN Department of Public Information, DPI 1033 40054. March, 1990.

14. The UN Law of the Sea Treaty: Can It Be Revived?

by Miriam Levering

The United Nations Convention on the Law of the Sea, signed by 159 nations and ratified by 45 out of the required 60 to bring it into force, has already, since 1982, been accepted by most nations, including the United States, as "customary international law." This comprehensive 1982 Treaty negotiated for some 15 years by consensus, was designed to prevent anarchy, conflict, and despoliation of three fifths of the Earth's surface, the oceans.

Its more than 400 articles, covering all aspects of ocean space and resources, while not perfect, advances peaceful settlement of disputes, environmental law, and international institution building, as well as freedoms and obligations at sea, beyond their 1982 levels. As a Constitution, it is the framework for ongoing efforts, treaties, and agreements which "fill in" the Treaty. It is the foundation on which negotiations on such issues as toxic waste, global warming, the pollution of regional seas, the destruction of coral reefs, of stocks of fish and marine mammals rest. It is basic to the 1992 UN Conference on Environment and Development. It is no accident that its President,

Ambassador T.T.B. Koh of Singapore, is chairing the preparations for that Conference in Brazil. This was recognized by the World Commission on Environment and Development as follows:

"The UN Conference on the Law of the Sea was the most ambitious attempt ever to provide an internationally agreed regime for the management of the oceans. The resulting Convention represents a major step towards an integrated management regime for the oceans . . . Indeed, the most significant initial action that nations can take in the interests of the oceans' threatened life support system is to ratify the Law of the Sea Convention."

Those who know it best were not exaggerating when they called the Convention "a monumental achievement" for world order. Americans can take patriotic pride in the leadership of our government under the Johnson, Nixon, Ford, and Carter administrations in this struggle for world law. Probably no nation has no more "hard headed" interests in the Treaty than our own.

U.S. Vital Interests

Senator Claiborne Pell, chairman of the Senate Foreign Relations Committee, is clear that the overriding interest of the United States is in the rule of law. Other vital interests include: the universally recognized freedoms of navigation and overflight for military and commercial ships and aircraft through and over international straits, 200 mile exclusive economic zones (EEZs), archipelagic waters, and the high seas; preservation of the global ocean commons and conservation of marine living species; rights to manage and duties to conserve ocean resources in the U.S. 200 mile EEZ and continental shelf; rights to conduct basic marine scientific research worldwide, now threatened by national ocean claims; universally recognized rights to mine the deep seabed under an International Seabed Authority; agreed mechanisms, often compulsory, for peaceful settlement of disputes ranging from mediation to judicial settlement; and U.S. leverage in global problem-solving and a stronger United Nations.

The LOS Convention already forms the basis of most oceans practice today. In late April, 1991, Rear Admiral William Schachte (USN), Deputy Judge Advocate General and Department of Defense Representative for Oceans Policy Affairs, called the Convention "a living document." He stated that the treaty "is used every day; it is the source of legal guidance provided in the Commanders Handbook on the Law of Naval Operations issued by the Department of Navy. Although basically a peacetime document, it has great value in promoting predictability and consensus on boundaries and navigation rights that cannot be suspended. . . . Iran, for example, did not even consider whether to obstruct vessels'

entry into the Persian Gulf." The U.S. and Soviet Union in 1989 confirmed the navigation provisions when they bumped each other in the Gulf in a "Uniform Interpretation" agreement.

This treaty is always consulted before legislation is drafted in the House Merchant Marine and Fisheries Committee, to assure its compliance with the LOS Treaty. National claims of territorial sea exceeding 12 miles have been rolled back.

Let a nation violate the non-seabed mining parts of this treaty, and it receives an official protest from the State Department. In fact, 118 protests have been filed since 1979 against 47 nations. Most of these protests deal with Treaty-forbidden national expansions in the ocean, usually called "creeping jurisdiction," and violations of transit rights of vessels. In one case, the U.S. cited the 1982 Convention in protesting the jailing of a U.S. tuna boat captain and his mate by Kirabatu, an island government in the South Seas.

Let a proposal emerge in Congress deviant from the LOS Convention's non-seabed parts, and the administration opposes it.

Readers of the Elliot Richardson-led Council on Ocean Law publications know that such UN bodies as the Inter-governmental Maritime Organization, the UN Environmental Program, and UNESCO's International Oceanic Commission regularly forge instruments and launch programs which not only fill in and implement the 1982 Convention, but also enhance UN efforts. Treaties and commissions to protect tuna and prevent pollution of the Mediterranean and Caribbean are vital to global life support systems today.

Seabed Management Problems

In fact, even in Part XI of the Treaty, the vexed system of management of the international seabed area, this "common heritage of mankind," whose fabled but economically non-viable lumps of nickel, copper, cobalt, and manganese lie three miles down on the ocean floor: the sole cause of the Reagan dropout and the Bush non-drop back into the Treaty completion and implementation process -- even here Treaty provisions are being carried out.

The Preparatory Commission charged with implementing Treaty institutions, such as the new International Seabed Authority with headquarters in Jamaica, and the Law of the Sea Tribunal to be set up in Hamburg, Germany, has drafted a seabed mining code in Part XI and has met nine times, virtually completing the non-divisive aspects of its work. The UN Secretary-General has registered four mine site claims by "Pioneer Investors." A fifth (from China) has been accepted by the Prepcom in 1991, and a sixth (from Cuba, Czechoslovakia, Poland, Bulgaria, and the USSR) has been submitted.

The Secretary-General of the UN himself has taken over the divisive issues in the mining system, all nine of them, for resolution. Three Consultations of representatives of about 45 states, including U.S. Ambassador Thomas Pickering, have occurred since 1990. These issues, relating to access to the Area by mining entities, who controls the international machinery, and who pays, are the sticky ones, not only for the U.S. but for other industrialized governments including the U.S.S.R. With widespread agreement that ocean mining is a long way off if ever, due largely to economic non-viability which has caused private consortia to shrink almost into oblivion, the Secretary-General's Consultations are wrestling with which problems to tackle and which to postpone.

They are racing the clock. In three years or so the Treaty could enter into force without Part XI having been made mutually satisfactory. U.S. refusal so far to participate is clearly the most depressing fact in the struggle. So far, pro-Treaty elements in the government have yet to persuade power centers like John Sununu, Richard Darman and Secretary Baker.

Does all of this activity indicate a feeble dying Treaty? Perhaps we have asked the wrong question. How about this question: Should the LOS Convention come into force?

As indicated above, here our answer could be NO. Not if the 60 nations ratifying do not include major industrialized nations. Now only one of the 45 is an industrialized nation, Iceland. And it is not a likely candidate for seabed mining. If the Treaty comes into force before industrialized nations have changed the seabed mining system, then they would be faced with a cumbersome, difficult amending process provided for in the Convention.

Let us change the question to: Can the LOS Convention enter into force with signatories from both the industrial and non-industrial states?

But first, some prior questions: If the U.S. government feels it is doing fine with the customary law status quo, with national legislation in place for eventual seabed mining, with a policy of continued pressure upon deviants, why help to bring the Convention into force? The answer lies in the following considerations.

* Customary international law is conflict-prone. Chile, for example, disagreed with our protest of its adding to its continental shelf unilaterally. We said it

acted contrary to Article 76 of the Convention which the U.S. recognizes as "customary international law." Chile, however, doubted if Article 76 ever was "customary international law." The fact that we have protested Treaty-deviant behavior 110 times indicates that customary law consensus is far from perfect and could erode further.

If we pick and choose among parts of the treaty the ones we like and will honor, others are encouraged thereby to do the same, and the consensus falls apart.

* Is President Bush serious about a new world order, or is it just a war slogan? If so, let him tell Baker, Darman, and Sununu that the rule of law comes first with him. He will opt for Treaty law with the fullest implementation of its provisions not only in navigation rights and boundaries, but also in the vital provisions of dispute settlement, ocean scientific research, and the protection of the oceans. Strengthening international law and institutions must come first.

There are three steps to effect a policy change:

1. That Part XI be changed satisfactorily to the U.S.

2. That the seabed mining industry accept the changes.

3. That the Right Wing abstain from attacking the Treaty.

* Can other industrialized nations forget the United States and proceed to amend Part XI and ratify the Convention? This is not impossible, and may be the final hope. Earlier, Germany seemed a strong possibility, but unification problems currently overwhelm that government. The thought of assuming financial burdens of the proposed International Seabed Authority without the United States impedes progress. The earlier expectation that imminent mining would fund the Authority has faded.

* Even with the political will, technically could the provisions of Part XI be changed in a treaty when 45 nations have already ratified?

Professor Louis Sohn and George Taft of the State Department's Treaty section agreed that it is possible legally and cited precedents where protocols were added altering the original Convention without Treaty ratification. In a paper read to the Center for Ocean Law and Policy of the University of Virginia's Law School on April 19-20, Professor Sohn reminded his hearers that the U.S. Constitution entered into effect "unconstitutionally" because of widespread recognition it needed to be amended (with a Bill of Rights) even before the Constitution went into effect.

Protocol Precedents

Professor Sohn cited as a more recent precedent involving the Intergovernmental Maritime Organization's Convention on the Prevention of Pollution from Ships, 1973/78. Here, the signatories substituted stronger provisions before the weaker ones entered into force. In the LOS case, the UN General Assembly could convene a special conference to develop a protocol incorporating the non-seabed provisions of the 1982 Convention and new provisions to make the seabed regime widely acceptable. The Protocol and Convention would be considered a single document, read and interpreted together. The application of certain provisions of the protocol could be delayed for a certain time or until circumstances trigger their effectiveness.

Professor Sohn also cited a second method of amending the Convention before it enters into force -- authentic interpretation. This provides a way to avoid modification of the Convention's text. A series of interpretative understandings could be included in a protocol and ratified with the Convention. This is not uncommon in overcoming obstacles to U.S. participation in international agreements.

Professor Sohn was clear. This is not a technical problem. The scholar drew on his least scholarly source -- the common adage, "Where there's a will, there's a way."

The United Nations Secretary-General and his Under Secretary clearly call upon the U.S. government to summon the will. In May 1991 Nandan said: "Despite the fact that the problems with Part XI have been generally recognized and others have begun to resolve these problems, with developing nations now sharing the views of the industrialized, the U.S. has refused to make a commitment to engage in detailed substantive negotiations."

The United States government is, after all, us. We must demand that our leaders stop talking about the difficulties and help overcome them. The executive branch seems frozen in extremist ideology and political fear. Congress, however, despite its overload of competing issues, offers hope. The place to begin is the House Merchant Marine and Fisheries Committee and the Senate Foreign Relations and Commerce Committees. The focus now, according to staffer Charles Moore of the House Merchant Marine and Fisheries Committee, should be on the Convention's environmental provisions. On global related issues, for example, the Administration's position has already been changed.

All the time honored techniques of influencing policy, all the personal and coalition activation, all the conviction and sustaining power are needed now. Without this effort, an inadequate Convention lacking the support of industrial nations, slow and difficult to change, could come into force.

Discussion Questions

1. Is the LOS Treaty with its International Seabed Authority an important element in a New World Order Under Law?

2. What is the best method of reviving the LOS Treaty?

3. Should the Treaty be amended to meet U.S. objections?

REFERENCES AND SUGGESTED READINGS

Ocean Policy News. Council on Ocean Law Newsletter. 1709 New York Avenue, NW, Suite 800, Washington, DC, 20006 "The United States and the 1982 Convention on the Law of the Sea." "Synopsis of the Status of the Treaty and its Expanded Role in the World Today."

The United Nations Convention of the Law of the Sea. United Nations, New York, 1982.

14. Human Rights --
How Can the Conventions Be Promoted and Enforced?

by Kathryn Damm

At what point should the UN intervene in the internal affairs of a member state to protect the human rights of an ethnic, racial or religious group? This question is fundamental to our discussion of human rights. State sovereignty has been viewed as the absolute authority, something untouchable because its very nature is the foundation of each country. Putting human rights in a system of international cooperation implies that human rights represent transboundary values and that whenever they are in jeopardy, the international community is entitled to raise it as a concern. We must then ask ourselves: At what point do concerns over human rights abuses override traditional concepts of state sovereignty?

With those questions in mind, let us examine what human rights are. Article one of the UN Charter proclaims, "We the

peoples of the UN determined . . . to reaffirm faith in fundamental human rights, in the dignity and worth of the human person, in the equal rights of men and women and of nations large and small . . ." Reinforcing that idea is a quotation from the Declaration of the Right to Development which states, "All human rights and fundamental freedoms are indivisible and interdependent; equal attention and urgent consideration should be given to the implementation, promotion and protection of civil, political, economic and social rights." These two quotations reveal a common theme: human rights of all persons must be protected and treated with care lest they be taken too lightly and then violated.

Universal Declaration

The General Assembly of the UN adopted the Universal Declaration of Human Rights in 1948. In twenty concise articles, it proclaims that all human beings are free and equal; that everyone has the right to life, liberty and security of person; that no one should be held in slavery; that all are equal before the law; and that no one shall be subject to arbitrary arrest, detention or exile. It also declares the right to a fair hearing; the presumption of innocence; the right to privacy; freedom of travel; the right to asylum; the right to marriage; the right to own property; freedom of thought, conscience and religion; freedom of opinion and expression; the right to peaceful assembly and association; the right to participate in government; the right to work; the right to an adequate standard of living; the right to an education; and the right to participate in the cultural life of the community. This was not intended to be legislation. Rather, it was the foundation on which treaties and covenants to implement the Declaration would be based. However, nobody foresaw how long implementation would be in coming and the problems it would bring to the UN.

Covenant on Economic, Social and Cultural Rights

To begin, there are at least seven major international human rights instruments used by the UN to set standards for human rights. The International Covenant on Economic, Social and Cultural Rights was opened for signature in 1966 and went into effect in 1976. In September 1990, ninety-five states had ratified this covenant. The U.S. has signed it but the Senate has not yet ratified it. The states ratifying this covenant undertake to promote the rights to work, to join a trade union, to have social security, to have an adequate standard of living, to have an education and to take part in cultural life.

Covenant on Civil and Political Rights

The International Covenant on Civil and Political Rights was also opened for signature in 1966 and went into effect in 1976. As of October 1990, ninety-two nations had ratified this covenant. Some topics addressed in the International Covenant include the right to self-determination, protection of persons subjected to detention or imprisonment, freedom of association, right to marriage, right to vote, freedom of religion, right to hold opinions, right to presumed innocence, and the right to due process.

The Covenant also created an eighteen person Human Rights Committee to receive and consider reports and communications filed by one signatory state regarding a dereliction of another signatory state. An Optional Protocol signed by some countries allows the committee to consider communications directly from individuals who claim to be victims of that country's actions.

An example of a case reviewed by the Human Rights Committee involved Paavo Muhonen vs. the country of Finland. Mr. Muhonen filed for conscientious objection to the Finnish law of mandatory military service on March 28, 1981. He requested alternative service and pleaded his case to the Finnish Military Service Exam Board, citing "a serious moral conviction against war." A Finnish court deemed his arguments implausible and six months later he was asked to report for service. He refused and submitted an appeal to the Ministry of Justice. He was furloughed for his failure to report for military service and given eleven months imprisonment. After serving five months, he was pardoned by the Committee under Article 18 of the Covenant which states, "Everyone shall have the right to freedom of thought, conscience and religion. This right shall include the freedom to have or adopt a religion or belief of his choice . . . and freedom either individually or in community with others and in public or private, to manifest his religion or belief in worship, observance, practice and teaching." However, he was not financially compensated for the five months he did serve, for the humiliation he suffered during the trial and numerous appeals. This decision by the Human Rights Committee under the Optional Protocol demonstrates the need to give the committee more jurisdiction into matters that protect individuals from states. Since it is neither a court nor a body with a quasi-judicial mandate, its decisions are described as "views", not "judgments".

Convention on Elimination of Racial Discrimination

The third convention is the International Convention on the Elimination of All Forms of Racial Discrimination. It was initiated in 1969 and as of August 1990, one hundred twenty-nine states had ratified it (including the U.S.). Some of the important points of this convention include: a) to encourage multiracial organizations as a means of eliminating barriers between races; b) that any doctrine of racial differentiation or superiority is scientifically false, morally condemnable and has no justification in theory and practice; c) that

government policies based on racial superiority or hatred violate fundamental human rights and endanger international peace and security; d) racial discrimination not only harms those who are its objects but those who practice it. This is the most ratified convention.

The convention declares that all states must submit periodic reports to CERD (Committee on Elimination of Racial Discrimination) provides for state-to-state complaints, and allows individuals to make complaints against their state (but only if their state is a party to the convention). CERD must then report to the U.N. General Assembly and the Secretary General. Two prominent problems are the failure (or extreme lateness) in paying dues agreed upon by state parties to support CERD and the failure to submit the reports on time or at all. This has caused some sessions to be canceled or finished early because of financial reasons.

Genocide and Apartheid Conventions

The Convention on the Prevention and Punishment of the Crime of Genocide was opened for signature in 1948, went into effect in 1961, and was finally ratified by the U.S. in 1986. It confirms that genocide is a crime under international law, defines genocide to include the killing or the causing of serious harm to members of a group with the intent to destroy in whole or in part a national, ethnic, racial or religious group. It mandates the punishment of persons committing genocide "whether they are constitutionally responsible rulers, public officials or private individuals." It also provides that persons charged with genocide shall be tried by a competent national tribunal where the act was committed or by an "international penal tribunal." (The U.S. Senate filed a reservation on the latter point.)

The International Convention on Suppression and Punishment of the Crime of Apartheid was put into effect in 1976. As of August 1990, 89 states had ratified this convention, although the U.S. has not. The Security Council in 1963 and 1977, to overcome the evil of apartheid in South Africa, imposed sanctions on sales of military equipment and justified this by saying that apartheid was a threat to international peace and security. While some laws have been revoked recently, more still needs to be done. In 1989, President F. W. de Klerk declared, ". . . only a negotiated understanding among the representative leaders of the entire population is able to insure lasting peace. The alternative is growing violence, tension and conflict." The real problem is that in this era peace is still not based on respect for human rights, but on maintaining a balance of economic, political and military power.

Conventions on Discrimination against Women and against Torture

The Convention on the Elimination of All Forms of Discrimination against women went into effect in 1980. As of June 1990, 103 states had ratified it (the U.S. has signed but not ratified it yet). This convention's importance lies in targeting an audience that has been discriminated against for centuries and parts of the world still find discrimination acceptable. Some provisions include: to take all appropriate measures to suppress all forms of exploitation, that maternity is a social function and common responsibility of men and women, and to modify the cultural patterns of men and women.

Lastly, the Convention against Torture and Other Cruel, Inhuman or Degrading Treatment or Punishment was initiated in 1984. As of June 1990, 52 states had ratified it (the U.S. has signed but not yet ratified). Torture is defined as any act by which severe pain or suffering, whether physical or mental, is intentionally inflicted on a person to obtain information or a confession. Some of its provisions include: abolition of corporal punishment in Trust Territories, standard minimum rules for the treatment of prisoners, protection against arbitrary arrest and detention and principles of medical ethics. An important clause notes that no state party may extradite a person to another state when there is grounds to believe he/she may be tortured. Non-governmental organizations play a critical role because they furnish information that governments sometimes deem "classified" to protect themselves. The UN Committee against Torture acts as a monitoring body to which the State parties regularly must submit reports. Two problems are the lack of financial resources needed to fully research every complaint and the need to set up the UN Voluntary Fund for Victims of Torture for those the UN was too late in helping.

Failure of Some States to Ratify

One general problem is the failure of nation states to ratify human rights covenants and conventions. Does this constitute a failure of the member nations or a failure of the U.N.? While the governments of each nation must do the ratifying, the UN and Secretary General in particular, could take the lead in developing a worldwide constituency on behalf of the Universal Declaration of Human Rights. Another problem is how much of these conventions are merely rhetoric? The key to that question lies in implementation and publicity. The machinery for human rights implementation must not be restricted to those areas in which the majority has a direct political interest. Thus, all human rights violations must be treated equally, for a man beaten to death in Chile is just as dead as a man beaten to death in South Africa.

Institutions Needed to Enforce Conventions

There are several international human rights institutions which are needed to help implement human rights conventions. An International Criminal Court, for example, could try individuals charged with the crime of genocide.

A proposed World Court on Human Rights could hear cases from areas that do not have a regional court, like the European Court of Human Rights which has been in existence for several years. There is also an American Court of Human Rights that the U.S. does not participate in.

A UN Electoral Monitoring Agency was proposed by George Bush last year. This concept is not new; the U.N. did it in Namibia, Haiti and Nicaragua. This idea assumes elections may not be fairly conducted without directly accusing the host nation of corruption. It could help insure the right to universal and equal suffrage spelled out in Article 25 of the Covenant on Civil and Political Rights.

A final human rights instrument that is needed is the UN High Commissioner for Human Rights, a proposal tabled by the General Assembly in 1978. The delegation from Costa Rica proposed it as a way to independently consider abuses on a global scale. President Carter endorsed it heartily, but it failed in the 32nd Assembly by a vote of 69-49 and was never reintroduced.

The key to successful protection of human rights lies in implementing existing conventions. In order to stop abuses, new and stronger institutions must be given the power to act with the full support of member nations. The Security Council was able to go beyond the traditional concept of state security with Kuwait to encompass the security of a group, the Kurds. Under a strengthened UN, human rights abuses will be less and if they occur, the perpetrators will be brought to the bar of justice.

Discussion Questions

1. Why shouldn't the U.S. ratify the two Human Rights Covenants and the Conventions on Apartheid, Torture and Against Discrimination against Women?

2. Why shouldn't the U.S. ratify the American Convention on Human Rights and participate in the American Court of Human Rights?

3. Should a UN Electoral Monitoring Agency be mandatory at all elections in member states or only when requested by the host country?

4. How should the Human Rights Conventions be enforced in a restructured United Nations?

5. What additional courts or other institutions are necessary in your view to implement and enforce the Human Rights Conventions?

REFERENCES AND SUGGESTED READINGS

Amnesty International--Torture in the 80's, Amnesty Int'l Publications. London, 1984.

Baratta, Joseph Preston. **Human Rights: Improving UN Mechanisms for Compliance.** May, 1990.

Biergental, Ted. **Implementing the UN Racial Convention.** Texas Int'l Law Journal, 1987.

Falk, R. **Human Rights and State Sovereignty,** Holmes and Meier, 1981.

Human Rights: A Compilation of International Instruments. Centre for Human Rights in Geneva, 1988.

Manual on Human Rights Reporting. World Campaign for Human Rights and by UNITAR, 1991.

Selected Decisions of the Human Rights Committee under Optional Protocol. Volume Two. October 1987-April 1988.

6

Part Four
ALTERNATIVE PATHS
TO A NEW WORLD ORDER

16. Two Visions:
U.S. Hegemony or World Equality Under Law

by Gerald Biesecker-Mast

"The rhetorical appeals to democracy and a new world order that have been heard in the Gulf War must not obscure the struggles for democratization and a just world order that so urgently remain before us," concludes Richard Falk in an article which laments the compromise of the UN system by the United States during the Gulf conflict. Falk believes that the "new world order" exemplified by the Gulf War is one in which the North exercises power over the South by maintaining a technology gap which prevents the wealthy nations from being imperiled by the poorer. "It is evident that the new world order as conceived in Washington is about control and surveillance, not about values or a better life

President Bush addressing the UN General Assembly, September 1990. UN photo 174426.

for the peoples of the world," according to Falk.

World Federalists historically share Falk's concern and have for decades envisioned a world order considerably different from the one Falk attributes to Washington. World Federalists have worked instead to achieve a peaceful world where international institutions mediate international disputes and where those institutions avoid simply reproducing the inequitable relations among the nations which have often led to war and always caused poverty and oppression. One of the greatest obstacles to this goal has been the impact of nationalism. Any world federalist approach to the new world order must consider the impact of

-102-

nationalism on international institutions. Nationalism has been called by some the most powerful ideology of our time. While a federalist version of internationalism need not be posited in opposition to nationalism, it certainly is opposed to some of its excesses. Federalists hesitate to justify internationalism primarily in terms of advancement of national interest.

In other words, attempts to advance the federalist cause must take under consideration how the balance of power, capital and natural resources in the world today might simply get reproduced within international institutions. World Federalists are interested not in advancing the interests of the powerful when they call for world governance; rather, they are concerned that all humanity be served by a just order. World Federalists have often explained their agenda in terms provided by Emery Reves back in 1945. Reves described the two alternative visions of world security as guided by either the principle of law or the principle of conquest. "As the nation state structure excludes a legal order embracing men living in different sovereign units, the drive for security directly produces the drive for conquest," Reves argued. Consequently, Reves believed that "the drive for security is the major cause of imperialism." The dichotomy between conquest and law, then, has for a long time been the means for World Federalists to distinguish their agenda from nationalists and imperialists. World law has been posited as an alternative to powerful nations pursuing unilateral aims at the expense of the weak.

New More Complicated Scenario

However, the World Federalist movement is presently confronted with a new, more complicated scenario: the international institutions in which it has invested so much work and hope have been used by a powerful world leader to legitimate a destructive war designated as an international effort, but undertaken largely as a unilateral action. New times call for new definitions. World Federalists today must be very specific about the content of their vision for a democratic world federation in order to distinguish it from the popular conception of international institutions which views them primarily as a means to advance the interests of the powerful nations.

As a way to update Emery Reves' observations, World Federalists might pose two alternatives for the pursuit of security within a new world order governed by international institutions: one would follow the principle of hegemony; the other would follow the principle of equality under law. The principle of hegemony seeks to advance a particular society's culture, politics, and values as a universal paradigm; whereas, the principle of equality under law seeks to make the world safe for cultural, political and social diversity. The principle of hegemony encourages one nation to lead the rest of the world to a peaceful future, but the principle of equality under law posits international structures as sites where all the nations enjoy an equitable position from which they can work to settle disputes peacefully and justly.

The principle of hegemony was described well by Jerry Sanders, writing in the Spring '91 *World Policy Journal*, as "the universalist illusion" spawned by the end of the Cold War and the allied victory in the Gulf which "interprets the collapse of communism as the final moral victory for the West -- the so-called end of history -- and the beginning of a new era of universal purpose inspired by the Western, and more specifically American model of politics and culture." The "universalist illusion" is illustrated in this comment by George Bush on May 15, 1991 to American servicemen at Maxwell Air Force Base in which he describes what a new world order does *not* mean for him:

> You see, as the Cold War drew to an end we saw the possibilities of a new world order in which nations worked together to promote peace and prosperity. I'm not talking here of a blueprint that will govern the conduct of nations or some supernatural structure or institution. The new world order does not mean surrendering our national sovereignty or forfeiting our interests. It really describes a responsibility imposed by our successes.

In this statement, Bush clearly rejects the idea of submitting to the authority of an international institution or responding to any principle higher than national sovereignty. Furthermore, he presents the role of the United States within the international political scene in a way which presumes the triumph of its values and implies the superiority of its political agenda. Contrary to this approach, World Federalists have always worked for a world where cultural, political, religious and social differences are respected and encouraged within a framework of enforceable world law.

How World Federalists Can Distinguish Hegemony from Egalitarianism

If World Federalists are to successfully promote a new world order under law, they must be prepared to identify the difference between a hegemonic world order and an egalitarian world at three different registers: (1) in conversations about the structure and function of the United Nations and its related agencies, (2) in the rhetorical strategies of President Bush and other political leaders which call forth an American political role in the world, and finally, (3) in World Federalist efforts to imagine a more just, more peaceful world in which nations are gathered in a united federation.

The discussion about the future of the UN reveals much about the commitments of its participants. Advocates of U.S. hegemony are reluctant to strengthen the position of the United Nations through reform; instead, they would rather take advantage of the UN's relative weakness by arbitrarily recognizing or refusing its authority depending on whether they believe the U.S. interest is served. Those who seek equality under law, on the other hand, believe that the interests of all peoples will be better served if the United Nations is fundamentally reformed or restructured to make it more difficult for even the most powerful states to abuse it. Perhaps the most telling evidence of the current President's lack of interest in reforming the United Nations is his failure to make his appointments to the U.S. Commission on Improving the Effectiveness of the UN, a commission established by Congress but which may be rendered inoperative by the President's delinquency. World Federalists and the members of many other organizations concerned about the future of the UN have repeatedly requested that the President make his appointments to no avail.

The problematic relation of the United Nations to the events in the Persian Gulf provides an important occasion for World Federalists to argue for UN reform along the lines required by the principle of

-104-

equality under law. The War in the Gulf revealed a number of weaknesses in the structure and process of the United Nations, weaknesses which resulted in the assertion of U.S. hegemony in the region rather than in successful mediation by international laws and institutions.

First of all, the UN Security Council gave insufficient attention to the escalating quarrel between Iraq and Kuwait over borderlines, port access and use of common natural resources. If the International Court of Justice had sufficient authority to adjudicate the dispute, the conflict might have been resolved peacefully. Additionally, a comprehensive international monitoring and information gathering system might have prompted the United Nations to intervene or at least carry on Security Council discussions before war broke out.

Secondly, the UN response to the invasion itself departed from procedures outlined in the Charter which place control for enforcement of UN resolutions under the control of the UN Security Council and the Military Staff Committee. The Security Council instead requested that individual nations monitor shipping in the Gulf and eventually authorized coalition members to use "all necessary means" against Iraq after January 15. As a result, the decisions about when to use military force, where to use it, and how much to use were all made by the U.S. strategic command rather than by an independent command structure appointed by the UN Security Council. World Federalists advocate a Security Council with peacekeeping, peacemaking, and enforcement powers. Such powers would probably require an active Military Staff Committee with authority to direct all operations of U.N. forces drawn from the forces of all UN members. In addition, the office of the Secretary-General should be restructured so that the Secretary-General has the means to monitor and recommend early intervention in situations threatening global security.

Thirdly, a strengthened UN can prevent human rights violations by adjudicating matters traditionally reserved for national governments. This expanded jurisdiction would include judgements on crimes against diplomats such as those perpetrated by Iraq against U.S. diplomats living in Iraq and authority to hold individuals accountable for their participation in torture and genocide. Increasingly, the plight of the Kurdish refugees and others like them who are displaced by civil wars and political conflict can be seen as a human rights concern which is only inadequately being addressed by unilateral action. Specifically, World Federalists support the establishment of a World Court of human rights which would hear and judge cases brought by individual world citizens against national governments and heads of state who are accused of human rights abuses. Relying on national governments to perform these actions only increases the possibility that responses to human rights violations will fall along politicized lines.

Fourthly, the environmental damage caused by the Gulf War is a tragic example of the destruction to the earth perpetrated by modern warfare. The United Nations Environmental Program presently only has power to monitor threats to the environment and to encourage efforts to improve it. World Federalists call for the transformation of the UNEP into a regulatory agency authorized to enforce global environmental standards. The increased authority and visibility of the UNEP could insure a global response to environmental concerns.

The limitations on effective UN responses to the Gulf War only confirm the urgency of a New World Order guided by World Federalist principles of equality under law. Prevention of tragedies like the Gulf War can only be effected by the transformation of the United Nations into a system of global security empowered to contain and arbitrate international disputes before they break into violent wars. If such a global security system is not established, the United Nations will continue to be ignored or manipulated by the most powerful nations at the expense of the weakest or frozen into inaction by disputes among the permanent members of the Security Council.

How the Bush "New World Order" Falls Short of Federalist Principles

Another political space in which World Federalists should exercise a critical voice is in public response to the efforts of President Bush to identify the American nation as the harbinger of a new world order in which peaceful mediation will prevail over violent conflict. World Federalists should insist that the U.N. be granted the authority and means to settle international disputes through UN sponsored teams of arbiters representing many nations.

In particular, World Federalists should become sensitive to rhetorical uses of highly regarded terms like freedom and democracy which may sometimes be used as code words for American political hegemony in the world. While World Federalists identify with those concepts as Americans, they should be cautious about attempts to represent other nations as either succeeding or failing to live up to those American ideals. Perhaps an example of the use of terms such as democracy and freedom to obscure the political realities within other nations is in popular representations by the Bush administration of El Salvador. Even though many observers claim the government of El Salvador has become more brutal and violent during the past several years, the Bush administration has continued to call it a democratic nation and to cite it as one of the many evidences that democracy and freedom were breaking out around the world. Closer to the events most Americans are concerned about these days is another questionable labelling: the continuing characterization by President Bush of Desert Storm as a campaign to liberate Kuwait, when in fact what was also being defended was an authoritarian regime with relatively few traces of democratic principles at work.

Finally, movements for freedom and democracy within the Soviet Union are both heralded and carefully held at a distance by the Bush administration. In many of these cases, questions remain as to whether independent republics would foster or threaten democracy in the region, but certainly the concerns and demands of these social movements must be taken seriously by the international community. The best possible method for working toward peace, justice and security in all of these circumstances is through the efforts of international institutions with the authority and the resources to become directly involved. However, to this writer the present administration appears to prefer to take matters into its own hands, live up to the "responsibilities imposed by its success," and use American post-war military and political clout to tidy up the world scene.

The world must be told that this is not the way of World Federalism. American World Federalists must be especially careful to separate their own agenda for a New World Order from the Bush administration's apparent attempt to organize the world around an American military hegemony. This does not mean World Federalists should avoid using the terms Bush uses to describe his foreign policy. It does mean that World Federalists must distinguish themselves from the Bush foreign policy by attaching content to those terms which advance their own agenda for a world order governed by global institutions.

A Federalist Vision of Full Equality Under Law

The third register at which World Federalists must identify and advocate a world order following the principle of equality under law is their own imaginative efforts to conceive of a world federation of nations peacefully coexisting within an organized world structure of law and government. As World Federalists continue to hold discussions among themselves about the kind of world they work for, they must continue to question the assumptions they themselves bring to the discussion. Three particular areas for consideration come to mind: 1) the role of the individual in the new world order; 2) the role of the new social movements within a world federation; 3) the uses of the American model of federalism as a means to justify a world model of federalism.

Too often it is easy to view the international landscape as a world of nations in which the primary responsibility of international institutions is to mediate between the nations and exercise jurisdiction over member states. This approach tends to neglect the oppression of individuals and social groups by various national governments. The principle of equality should extend not only to nations, but to individuals and social groupings as well.

Already the World Federalist Movement has recognized the importance of internationalizing human rights. In a recent booklet published by the WFM, the authors support current efforts to give individuals standing before international bodies which are granted authority to intervene with national governments on behalf of individual citizens. The booklet encourages the reconstitution of the Trusteeship Council of the United Nations as a "Human Rights and Trusteeship Council," and advocates the establishment of "regional commissions and a United Nations High Commissioner as 'ombudsperson' empowered to investigate complaints of violations of such rights, together with regional and world courts of human rights permitting appeals directly by individuals".

Little attention seems to have been paid, however, to the place within federalism of the concerns and interests expressed by various social movements for equality, dignity and freedom. According to a number of thinkers in the area of international studies, critical social movements must be given recognition as significant political efforts to bring about social and global change, to cultivate the practice of global citizenship and to demand the recognition of equality and diversity. If this is true, World Federalists must pay increasing attention to feminists, racial minority movements, environmentalists, and anti-war groups, as well as the movements for national independence and democracy in Eastern Europe and Latin America. It is not clear how a model of federalism can adequately respond to social groups with no standing as a nation state; however, a federalism that seeks justice and equality must address itself to the injustices which spawn social movements.

This leads us to a final question concerning the assumptions behind our own movement: what is the effect of representing the agenda for World Federation as an American agenda with a grounding in historic American federalism? This strategy has worked to make sense of World Federalism to many Americans and therefore should not be questioned lightly. But it does seem possible that such a rhetorical strategy could be mistaken for another form of American triumphalism, a new way to assert American forms of governance as the universal good. World Federalists are not striving to impose American forms of governance on the rest of the world; but they are certainly influenced by their own culture in their imagination of what a "good" and effective world government would look like. Perhaps a fruitful comparison could be made between American federalism and the newest emerging form of large scale federalism on the international political scene: the European Community. What are the strengths and weaknesses of each? What has been overlooked and neglected in both models? Raising and discussing such questions would help insure that American World Federalists avoid the inadvertent advocacy of any form of American political hegemony.

Discussion Questions

1. Are the terms hegemony and equality adequate to describe the alternative visions of world order before us?

2. Should the rhetorical strategies of the World Federalists emphasize the areas in which Federalism is on common ground with the goals of the Bush administration or should it emphasize the differences?

3. How can the concerns of various global social movements, including various feminist, racial minority, and pro-democracy movements be addressed by World Federalists?

4. Should World Federalists continue to use the American model of federalism as a metaphor, if not an exact paradigm, for the World Federation of nations they are working to build?

5. How can a World Federalist agenda give sufficient attention to the concerns of individuals within the global family of nations?

6. Are there ways of preventing powerful world leaders from exploiting the United Nations to legitimate unilateral policy objectives?

7. How might the use of the United Nations by President Bush be turned to the advantage of political leaders who have a World Federalist agenda?

REFERENCES AND SUGGESTED READINGS

Beres, Louis R. **People, States, and World Order**. Itasca, IL: F.E. Peacock, 1981.

Falk, Richard. "Reflections on Democracy and the Gulf War." **Alternatives** 16 (1991) 263-274.

Mead, Walter R. "The Bush Administration and the New World Order." **World Policy Journal** 8 (1991) 375-420.

Reves, Emery. **The Anatomy of Peace.** Gloucester: Peter Smith, 1969.

Sander, Jerry. "Retreat From World Order." **World Policy Journal** 8 (1991) 227-250.

Tetreault, Mary Ann. "Regimes and Liberal World Orders." **Alternatives** 13 (1988) 5-26.

Walker, R.B.J. **One World, Many Worlds: Struggles for a Just World Peace.** Boulder, Colorado: Lynne Reinner Publishers, 1988.

World Association for World Federation. **World Federalism Today.** Amsterdam: WAWF, 1988.

17. The Building Block Approach to a New World Order

by Barbara Walker

Richard Falk's book <u>This Endangered Planet</u> contains a chapter, "Designing a New World Order System," where he suggests "a guideline for thought about an adequate world-order system. What we need to do is to concentrate upon design, not as a static image of a closed system but as an active process of learning and building; the idea of design includes the process of building over a long period of time, cathedral building in the sense of sustaining a large vision and embellishing on a basic plan of action as the occasion allows. . . ."

Let us work out practical paths which can be effective in the world today and not bog down inventing unlikely paths. We cannot predict the shape of the New World Order or how what we aspire to, might be achieved. It is important to consider what is going on in some key areas in the world today -- United Nations, National Sovereignty, European Community,

Environment and Development -- which may help point out the best route towards a New World Order.

Brian Urquhart, a retired Under Secretary of the United Nations in "Learning from the Gulf" in the <u>New York Review</u>, points out that "it is urgently necessary to consider what system of collective security will be best suited to the conflicts and forms of dangerous instability that are likely to arise in the future. No one nation, or even a partnership of two or three powerful nations, is going to be able to assume the role of world arbitrator and policeman. The United Nations must be brought to maturity to take that role." Robert Muller for many years an Assistant Secretary-General to the United Nations, thinks a strengthened United Nations will be necessary. "If the system doesn't work, nations will be in deep trouble."

Stanley Foundation Proposals for 1991

It is of paramount importance to empower existing institutions (the UN) as well as develop ideas for new structures. A recent Stanley Foundation annual conference saw four ways UN reform might be achieved this year: a stronger selection process for the Secretary General; reorganization of the Secretariat; repair work to make the "World's Meeting Place," the General Assembly, more effective; and redefinition and activation of the UN's role in economic and social affairs.

It is all very well to say we can do it through the UN, make it behave as it was supposed to, etc. But in examining issues, we often come upon the stumbling block of "national sovereignty." However, here there may be some cracks. A recent William Pfaff column for the Los Angeles Times Syndicate, "But Traditional Sovereignty Is Losing Its Luster," notes that leading democratic nations have taken it upon themselves to intervene in cases of humanitarian concern within the frontiers of sovereign states, and democracies argue that they have a right to protect national groups or to save people from their ancestral hatreds and communal follies. Thus the time has arrived to reconsider sovereignty's rights and limits. In our time the validity of the principle of national sovereignty has been challenged by communications technology, pollution, radioactive debris, the flow of money, the power of religious or secular ideas, AIDS, the traffic in drugs and terrorism. And the most obvious challenge, that of armaments, both nuclear and conventional, was addressed in 1989 by the Palme Commission on Disarmament and Security issues. Their final statement pointed out that traditional concepts of national security are obsolete, that all states depend on the good sense and restraint of others, that even opponents have a shared interest in survival. Thus true security depends on a partnership in the struggle against war.

The Example of European Integration

The process of European integration provides an example of eroding national sovereignty. Ferdinand Kinsky, Director of the Centre International de Formacion Europeenne, wrote in the 1986 **World Federalist News**: "The desire for peace amongst European nations after World War II . . . and the hope for greater independence from the United States of America, as well as the advantages of a larger market, were the major reasons for the difficult, but permanent and steady advance of European integration. Some of

The Palais de l'Europe, where the European Parliament holds its monthly plenary sessions, Strasbourg, France. Photo, Commission of the European Community.

the institutional arrangements in the European organizations are . . . at least pre-federalist." Most citizens of the Council of Europe are guaranteed their human rights by the possibility to go to a European Court. And the twelve common market countries have already transferred part of their sovereignty. Now monetary union is under consideration. The European Community has been seen as a model for other regions and, as a process, eventually for the world.

It may be that the fastest way toward stronger world legal and political institutions for the prevention of war is to make progress on global environmental management. The World Federalist Movement is working as coordinating organization for the NGO Task group on international institutions and legal matters, preparing positions for the UN Conference on Environment and Development to take place in Brazil next June.

The Stockholm Initiative on Development and Environment

The Stockholm Initiative on Global Security and Governance lays out specific proposals in the areas of Development and Environment: "DEVELOPMENT We propose: (8) that the world community sets the goal to eradicate extreme poverty within the coming 25 years, through a committed effort to achieve sustainable development; (9) that the following targets for the year 2000 be emphasized and that countries' achievements be monitored closely -- primary education for all children -- equal participation of boys and girls in schools -- reduction of child mortality by at least one third -- reduction in maternal mortality by one half; (10) a strengthening of the multilateral framework of trade-related agreements, reducing protectionism on all fronts, and expanding opportunities for developing countries' participation in world trade; (11) a strengthened debt strategy, introducing a strong element of debt forgiveness to radically curb the debt

overhang; (12) that all industrialized nations set public time-targets to provide one percent of their GNP for international development cooperation.
ENVIRONMENT We propose: (13) that fees are levied on the emission of pollutants affecting the global environment. In particular, carbon dioxide emissions from the burning of fossil fuels; (14) an international energy dialogue promoting a more efficient use of the world's energy resources, and, in particular, the use of alternative and renewable energy sources, e.g., solar energy; (15) that the United Nations be encouraged to take up environmental issues at the highest level in all appropriate fora; (16) that nations resolve to make the 1992 United Nations Conference on Environment and Development a breakthrough for achieving sustainable development."

New Global Structures Analogy

The European Community began with the European Coal and Steel Community in 1951 with the signing of the Treaty of Paris and culminated in 1986 with the Single European Act. Along the way many new structures were created including the Common Market, the European Monetary System and the European Parliament.

If we apply that model to the world at large, we might envisage a new and much stronger UN Environment and Development Authority emerging out of the 1992 Brazil Conference, followed later by a UN Verification system, a UN Peacekeeping Reserve, an International Criminal Court, and the gradual transformation of the General Assembly into a global parliament. These new global structures might culminate eventually into a new all encompassing UN

Flag of European Community

Charter establishing a world federation.

If we use the Richard Falk quote at the beginning of this article as a guide, we must develop our plans of action to fit occasions arising which support a "larger vision." Development of new structures will not come about except as solutions to existing situations. New structures must be agreed on by the world's negotiating parties, leaders, and so forth. We on the sidelines are not the actors to bring it about, but we can persevere in spreading our ideas with clarity and understanding.

Jean Monnet, Frenchman, architect of European integration writes in his <u>Memoires</u> of a list of principles he made for himself to guide him day by day. These principles end with, "It cannot all be done at once; it is gradually that we shall achieve this organization. . . . It is not a question of solving political problems which, as in the past, divide forces that seek domination or superiority. It is a question of inducing civilization to make fresh progress by beginning to change the form of the relationship between countries and by applying the principle of equality between peoples and between countries. . . . People no longer want their future to depend on the skill or ambition of their Governments.

They do not want ephemeral solutions, and, for that reason, they want there to be established in our countries an organization, a procedure, that will make possible collective discussion and decision."

Discussion Questions

1. Is a new UN Charter achievable in the foreseeable future?

2. Is it possible to make the UN more relevant to the industrialized countries? to the developing countries?

3. Many talk of reasons for erosion of national sovereignty. What steps can be taken to move this process?

4. Is the European Community process a practical model for the world?

5. Are the Stockholm Initiative proposals on ENVIRONMENT and DEVELOPMENT possible of achievement?

6. Are New Global Structures the best Route to a New World Order?

REFERENCES & SUGGESTED READINGS

The Economist. "Another Chance for the UN," February 23, 1991. "Plotting Monetary Union," May 19, 1990. "Renaissance on the East River," December 15, 1990. "The World Order Changeth," June 22-28, 1991.

Falk, Richard. "Designing a New World Order System." **This Endangered Planet.** Random House: New York, 1971.

Muller, Robert. **World Security for the 21st Century.** Benjamin Ferencz, editor. Oceana Publishers: New York, 1991.

Pfaff, William. **Los Angeles Times Syndicate.** July 1991.

Ramphal, Sir Shridath. "Making Human Society a Civilized State." **1987 Corbishley Memorial Lecture.** The Wyndham Place Trust: London.

Roosevelt, Eleanor. **Tomorrow Is Now.** Harper and Row: New York, 1961.

The Stanley Foundation Courier. Muscatine, Iowa: No. 7, Spring 1991.

"Summary of Proposals: Common Responsibility in the 1990's." **The Stockholm Initiative on Global Security and Governance.** April 22, 1991.

UN Document. "Final Statement of the Palme Commission on Disarmament and Security Issues." Stockholm, April 14, 1989. A/44/293/S/20653.

Urquhart, Brian. "Learning from the Gulf." **New York Review,** February 1991. "Sovereignty vs. Suffering." **New York Times,** April 21, 1991.

Whitehead, John and Jeffrey Laurenti. "The Hydra-Headed UN." **The Christian Science Monitor.** May 22, 1991.

18. The New UN Charter Approach for Achieving World Federation

by John Logue

In the midst of the Civil War Abraham Lincoln said that "the dogmas of the quiet past are inadequate to the stormy present. We must think anew and act anew." Recent world developments give world federalists a great opportunity to win support for their goal. But to take full advantage of that opportunity we must rethink our basic strategy.

In this brief essay I will contend that world federalists should put most of their programming, funding and staff time into a holistic approach to our goal. That goal is to achieve a United Nations world federation with the power, authority and funding to achieve the basic purposes of the United Nations, i.e. peace and security, protection of the global environment, promotion of economic and social progress and human rights. I will urge that the best constitutional strategy (defined below) to take is to urge the drafting and ratification of a new UN Charter and the best promotional strategy to take is a combination of techniques and projects we have used for other purposes.

The Holistic Approach to UN Reform and Restructure

Our Founding Fathers took a holistic approach to the job of launching a U.S. federation. In my view, their "all at once" strategy is much more relevant to the launching of a UN world federation than the functional or gradual strategy which Europeans have been using to build a European Federation. The European analogy has deeply influenced the thinking of many world federalists, other peace groups, academia and the media. Below I will say why I think it has less to say to us than the Philadelphia analogy and the holistic approach which it exemplified.

The holistic approach is based on a paradox, i.e. that it is sometimes easier to build a whole, in this case a UN world federation, than to build parts, i.e. separate workable parts. This is true because most of the parts of a world federation--whether an International Criminal Court or enforceable international law or "general and complete disarmament" or effective international environmental conventions or a more equitable system of decision-making--will not work adequately without the other parts and therefore will not be adopted without those other parts. Thus our common sense tells us that Saddam Hussein is not going to turn Saddam Hussein over to a powerless International Criminal Court and the United States is not going to extradite Ronald Reagan for mining the harbors of Nicaragua. And an empowered International Criminal Court implies the existence of a world federation.

To some the holistic approach is utopian. Yet it reflects the basic insight of world federalism, i.e. that projects like those I have mentioned are so interdependent that it is much easier to get

all of them--in a UN world federation--than any one of them by itself.

The Philadelphia Analogy

The example of the Founding Fathers is most instructive. Instead of proceeding sequentially, one step at a time, the Founding Fathers proceeded holistically, drafting a comprehensive Constitution and campaigning for its adoption. That Constitution included empowerment of a new federal government, a new scheme of representation, adequate and dependable financing, enforcement of federal law on the individual, and limitation of federal power by constitutional text, and by checks and balances among federal institutions. (We need all those things, and more, in a revised UN Charter or a new UN Charter.) The U.S. Constitution also provided a system for its adoption, i.e. approval by popularly elected ratifying conventions in any nine (out of thirteen) states. A similar provision will be necessary if we take the path of a new UN Charter. (See below.)

The success of the Founding Fathers demonstrated that it is often easier to negotiate and win agreement for a package of reforms, a package in which everybody wins something and everybody loses something, than to win agreement on a sequence of proposals, one by one. The Founding Fathers understood this.

They also understood that it is much easier to focus public attention on the negotiation of one comprehensive proposal and the fight for its adoption than on the drafting and adoption, sequentially, of a dozen small proposals. Madison and Hamilton realized that while they could hope to get giants like Washington and Franklin to participate in the holistic Convention they were planning for Independence Hall they could not hope to involve them--and their prestige--in a series of independent negotiations on a dozen particular problems. They knew that the participation of these-- and lesser--giants in the drama they were planning would generate great interest in the Constitution they hoped to draft there. They knew that the signatures of these famous men on that document would help to win public support for the bold and comprehensive package of reforms which they were contemplating.

The holistic approach to world federation urges that we devote much more of our staff time, funding and programming to a constitutional strategy and a promotional strategy.

George Washington chairing U.S. Constitutional Convention

Both of these strategies were approved by the WFA Board in the "Strategy for the Nineties" Statement it adopted in April 1989. These strategies must be coordinated with each other. Work on them by the national office must also be coordinated with work on them by local chapters.

Constitutional Strategies for a New UN

Our constitutional strategy should focus our own and public attention on three possible paths for getting a new United Nations: 1) Urge a responsible group to draft a new UN Charter, including a vetoless method of ratifying it; 2) Secure agreement on a comprehensive package of amendments to the existing UN Charter and ratification of those amendments by the process provided in that Charter; 3) Organize a popularly elected world constituent assembly to propose a new UN Charter, including a method of ratifying it. While we should continue to welcome all three approaches to getting a new United Nations we should, in my judgment, put most of our emphasis on one of them, i.e., the "New UN Charter" strategy. Here are some comments on each of the three approaches.

1. A New UN Charter. This strategy calls for the drafting of a new United Nations Charter by a "responsible body" and the ratification of that new Charter by a high portion of the present members of the United Nations, whether by national legislatures or by national

referendums. I suggest the appropriate portion for adoption of the new UN Charter should be 2/3 of all present UN members and 3/4 of all members having (50?) (100?) million people. However, no nation should have a veto on the ratification of the new Charter and its coming into effect.

The "responsible body" who would draft the new Charter should, it seems to me, be a group of twenty or so former presidents, prime ministers and other eminent persons, drawn from every region of the world. That is the kind of body implied in the April 1991 "Stockholm Statement", endorsed by many prominent world leaders. In Proposal 28 those leaders recommended, "as a matter of priority, the establishment of an independent International Commission on Global Governance." A similar approach is taken in the ICSUN Project. The Common Heritage Institute originated this call for the establishment of an International Commission on Strengthening the United Nations and involved many prominent and not so prominent persons in discussion of it. The late Norman Cousins served as Facilitator of the project. A (90-page) ICSUN Prospectus makes a good case for adopting a new UN Charter but suggests that serious attention should also be given to drafting and promoting a package of amendments to the existing UN Charter.

The core of the proposed Independent Commission could be self-appointed, as with the Brandt and Palme Commissions, or it could be appointed by the UN Secretary-General, as with the Brundtland Commission. As some of the commissions have done, it could meet in nine short sessions, three months apart, in nine different regions of the world. Or it could meet in one long session, e.g. for six months, with two or three two-week breaks.

It would certainly require a competent staff. It might well want to have--or authorize--regional hearings to get action proposals and it might want to encourage the formation of national bodies like the U.S. Commission on Improving the Effectiveness of the UN to hold their own hearings, make their own recommendations, and pass them on to the Independent Commission.

There is much to be said for providing for popular ratification of the new Charter, possibly in UN-observed elections. It certainly would give the new Charter more legitimacy than governmental or legislative ratification. Needless to say, any national government or legislature could prevent the holding of such elections. But, for many reasons they might prefer not to vote on it but rather to "pass the buck" to their people.

The idea of a new UN Charter--a replacement Charter--is a sensible and conservative idea. Many nations have used it, e.g., the U.S. in 1787, France in 1946 and 1958, Germany, Japan, Italy, the Soviet Union. The UN Charter is a replacement Charter for the League of Nations Covenant. When one attempts to amend an existing Charter one is almost forced to be timid and narrow-minded. When one drafts a new Charter one can be bolder but, at the same time, more sensitive to the interdependence of the many parts of the Charter. One wants to draft a Charter which is attractive but one which is also workable and acceptable. Zealots need not apply!

2. Amending the Existing UN Charter with a Comprehensive Amendment Package. This approach may be more acceptable to national governments and to some top leaders in the UN. Yet the major reason for its appeal, that Charter amendments are vetoable by any one of the Permanent Members of the Security

Council, is its major weakness. That weakness makes many individuals, organizations and governments reluctant to invest much time on the amendment package approach. They are also aware that amendment drafters would almost certainly be appointees of their governments and removable by them and, thus, would be on a tight leash.

The General Assembly's Committee on the Charter and Strengthening the Role of the Organization might be asked to come up with the necessary comprehensive package of amendments. However in its long years of existence that Committee has been very timid about proposing Charter amendments. A 1995 UN Charter Review Conference, as recently proposed by Parliamentarians for Global Action, might well be a high profile assembly, but it would still be faced with a number of the limitations listed above, especially the implications of the Great Power veto.

3. _A Popularly Elected World Constituent Assembly_. This approach has an honored place in the history of the world federalist movement. Unfortunately it has often, and quite unnecessarily, been associated with the idea of replacing the United Nations organization and not just the United Nations Charter. This is most unfortunate for there is no reason why a world federation should not, if at all possible, build upon the existing United Nations and its many find accomplishments, keep its honored name and fly its beautiful flag.

The relative lack of support for the world constituent assembly approach among contemporary world federalists reflects the many difficulties implicit in this approach, e.g. the difficulty of arranging free and fair elections without the help and even against the opposition of many national governments; the necessity of deciding, in advance, the controversial question of how many votes each nation is entitled to in the constituent assembly; the financing of the project; speculation as to whether many prominent persons will be elected to the assembly; speculation as to whether it will come up with a reasonably desirable, acceptable, and workable world constitution; the chances that national governments will permit and help administer free and fair elections; the chances that national governments, large or small, will feel bound to accept the judgment of the world's people, especially if their own people have voted against the world constitution. World federalists must be at least as much interested in substance, i.e., the structures, powers and safeguards of a world federation as in the procedure by which it is brought into existence.

A Promotional Strategy for a United Nations

One of the reasons why world federalists must seek agreement on a constitutional strategy is that it will permit them to focus their limited resources in an appropriate and effective promotional strategy. Thus if we agree that we want a new UN Charter and that that Charter should be drafted by an Independent Commission on Strengthening the United Nations or an International Commission on Global Governance we can design programs and strategies which will help bring those groups into existence and help them to succeed.

WFA played a key role in drafting and promoting the legislation which created the U.S. Commission on Improving the Effectiveness of the UN, promoted candidates for appointment to that Commission and raised substantial funding for the Commission. It has been urging the Commission to begin its work, with or without President Bush's not-yet-appointed appointees. WFA can and should perform the same functions with respect to the proposed independent International Commission on Global Governance. Obviously we will have to network with other organizations, not only in the United States but in many other countries. It is a good sign that the recent (quadrennial) World Congress of the World Federalist Movement (formerly WAWF) strongly endorsed the Stockholm Statement's proposal for an independent International Commission on Global Governance.

We can and must design appropriate literature, make videos, hold relevant meetings, introduce new sense resolutions, draft appropriate petitions, target key groups and audiences, organize and/or take part in parades and other demonstrations, these and a thousand other things. We can and must design federalist--and community--seminars and correspondence courses which will help local WFA chapters and other peace groups play a more effective role in support of our strategy. We can and must network effectively with non-federalist groups who are sympathetic with our goals but not yet persuaded of the need for the strategies that we believe are essential to reach those goals. We should continue to work for and support current WFA programs, such as an International Criminal Court, but with a smaller proportion of our precious resources and more stress on their interdependence with other programs and with the achievement of a world federation.

While we move forward--and in order to help us move forward--we must also go back to basics, i.e. become more familiar with basic world federalist concepts and writings, and encourage the writing and publication of new tracts, essays, articles and books. We must make a major effort to take our message to college and university campuses, in the United States and in as many other countries as possible. Our purpose should be not only to recruit new members but also and especially to influence the thinking and action of students and that of their professors.

A Footnote on the European Analogy

All of us are, to some extent, the slaves of analogies. The analogy of (appeasement at) Munich helped support the U.S. containment policy in Europe and in Korea. It also, unfortunately, influenced us to apply that policy to Vietnam. The Vietnam analogy influenced us to go into Iraq with massive power too quickly and to pull out too quickly. The problem persists and may do so for a long time. The European analogy is said to teach us that federations should be built gradually, one step at a time, beginning with less sensitive matters, such as a common market, and moving toward a common foreign policy and defense policy and institutions which can make and apply that common policy without interference by national governments. But that is not at all what happened in Western Europe in the years since World War II. The movement toward Western European unity and federation began with absolute security because of the presence of U.S. troops who were going to stay. The presence of those troops and their willingness to keep the peace permitted French and German political leaders to take bold initiatives at reconciliation and

-118-

cooperation that would not have been possible without them.

Indeed one of the difficulties which the European analogy has to explain is why the American Founding Fathers, who had so very much in common, felt they must move fast and holistically while the nations of Western Europe, who had been killing each other so recently, could afford to take their time about unification. The answer is that the Western European nations were and felt secure from their Western European neighbors as well as from the Soviet Union. But the thirteen American states felt threatened not only by many problems among themselves but also and especially by the English, the Spanish, the Indians and, to some extent, the French. They decided that their peace and their prosperity depended on their forming a more perfect Union as soon as possible. And so they did!

The world is threatened by many crises. It is essential that it move quickly and holistically toward a comprehensive solution to its problems, i.e. UN world federation. World federalists must show the way.

Discussion Questions

1. Is it easier to achieve a UN world federation by championing a series of partial reforms in the UN or by championing comprehensive, "all at once", reforms? Is there some "combination" or "middle way" between these two strategies?

2. Should comprehensive changes in the UN Charter be sought by calling a UN Charter Review Conference under Article 109 requiring ratification of amendments by all five of the Permanent Members of the Security Council, or would it be better to have a new UN Charter to be ratified by a large majority, but no veto?

3. If a new UN Charter is a good idea, who should draft it: A committee appointed by the General Assembly? An Independent Commission of eminent persons whose core members are appointed by the UN Secretary-General? A Commission appointed independently?

4. Is it practical to try to organize a popularly elected World Constituent Assembly to write a World Constitution to replace the UN Charter?

REFERENCES AND SUGGESTED READINGS

Adler, Mortimer J. **How to Think about War and Peace.** Simon and Schuster, 1944.

Borgese, G. A., etc. "A Preliminary Draft of a World Constitution". University of Chicago Press, 1947.

Clark, Grenville, and Sohn, Louis. **World Peace through World Law,** Second Edition, (Revised) Harvard University Press, 1966: Two Alternative Plans.

Hamilton, Alexander, Jay, John, and Madison, James. **The Federalist Papers.**

Logue, John. **The Great Debate on Charter Reform: A Proposal for a Stronger United Nations.** Fordham University Press, 1958.

Reves, Emery. **The Anatomy of Peace,** Eighth Edition, 1945-46. Harper & Brothers.

Walker, Barbara, ed. **World Federalist Reader 1: On the Bicentennial of the U.S. Constitution,** 1991.

Editor's Note: The strategy to achieve a UN World Federation may not be an "either/or" situation. The current five year plan of WFA (1990-95) employs both the New Global Structures Strategy referred to in Chapter 17 and the New UN Charter strategy described in Chapter 18. In addition, WFA is employing a strategy to increase planetary consciousness and to develop the growth of the World Federalist Movement.

19. Humanity's Most Pressing Need: World Federation

By John Holden

"The biggest lesson of all to be learned about contemporary civilization is that nothing anyone is doing today makes any sense unless it is connected to the making of a genuine peace." -- Norman Cousins.

Everyone is for world peace, but no one does very much about it. Although we continue to develop missiles, nuclear bombs and other sophisticated weaponry, we fail to realize that force and war are no longer viable alternatives to settling conflicts by peaceful means.

Our President says that we are the strongest and most powerful nation in the world -- the only country that could deliver sufficient force and manpower to the Gulf Region to enable the nations of the world to stand up to the Iraqi expansion into Kuwait. We spent billions of dollars a year preparing for war and we spent a billion a day to fight the war, while on the homefront we were unable to provide many of our own citizens with their basic needs, not to mention the rest of the people of the world. We lack both funds and motivation to stop the deterioration of our metropolitan and industrial infrastructure and to control damage that we are inflicting on our environment.

The Solution

The real solution to our problems (and perhaps the only solution) is the formation of democratic world federation -- a government of people as well as a government of nations. Such a government could be patterned after the U.S. constitution or possibly the European Community; it would require executive, legislative and judicial branches and would operate under a new UN Charter. We need to develop such a world federal government in order to handle global problems, including international warfare, environmental deterioration and human rights abuses.

The total picture presents increasing frustration. Too many people, considering the vast problems we face, think that they can do nothing; that our current problems are unsolvable.

What is lacking is individual accountability for criminal international actions. Under world federation international lawbreakers (such as terrorists, drug smugglers) would have no sanctuary but be brought to justice. World law would be enforced against the individual, not against entire nations.

World federation would grant only limited and specific powers to a central authority. Individual countries would exercise complete sovereignty over their own internal affairs. Under such a system, laws for solving global problems would be made by a legislative body such as a world parliament and international disputes between nations would be arbitrated by regional branches of the World Court and appealed to the World Court itself.

World federation would provide enforceable global laws to regulate interactions between nations. Safeguards such as a Constitutional Bill of Rights would

be built in to limit central government power.' As in our U.S. system of checks and balances, safeguards would prevent the possibility of totalitarian rule.

As Emery Reves said in The Anatomy of Peace: "Even those who, swayed by the logic of history or the eloquence of current events, see the importance of world government are likely to nod their heads and say, "Of course world government is the goal. But we can't get it immediately; we must proceed step by step."

Such a view overlooks the dire urgency of the problem. There is now no such thing as the first step toward world government. World government is the first step -- the step that must be taken before there is any chance of meeting other problems, economic and social. These problems will continue to exist, but the establishment of actual law rather than treaties among nations is essential to provide the framework and mechanisms through which these problems can be attacked.

The fundamental problem of regulating the relations between great powers without the permanent danger of major wars cannot be solved permanently so long as absolute power continues to reside in nation-states.

The most disconcerting of all objections is the assertion made by so many "public figures": "The people are not yet ready for world federation." One can only wonder how they know. Have they themselves ever advocated world federation? Have they ever tried to explain to the people what makes war and what is the mechanism of peace in human society? And, after having understood the problem, have the people rejected the solution and decided they did not want peace through law and government, but preferred war and unlimited national sovereignty?

Imagine a day in the future. Imagine that world federation was achieved years ago by amending the UN Charter or through an historic global constitutional convention. The idea of war between nations has now become as unthinkable as war between Missouri and Illinois. Fear of aggression has been eliminated. International conflicts are now settled in world courts of law. Maintaining national armies is unnecessary. Members of an international police force composed of multiple nationalities are strategically located throughout the globe. Through international regulation, transnational pollution has been eliminated.

Conclusion

As Theilhard de Chardin said, "A new world order should not be just an agenda item. We must develop a rhetoric that transcends politics and advances some such proposition as 'To think, feel and act as a global citizen is the essence of human survival.'"

Discussion Questions

1. What are you doing now for world peace? What can you do?

2. Do you believe a democratic world federation is the only solution to our global problems? What other solution do you propose?

3. In your view, are the people ready for world federation? What must be done to make them "ready"?

4. Can you describe how world federation will function after it is achieved?